MARCO POLO

Travel with
★ **Insider**
Tips

SO-ACY-938

TURKEY

UKRAINE

ROM.   RUSSIA

BULGARIA   *Black Sea*   GEORGIA

Istanbul   ARMEN.

Izmir   Ankara

T U R K E Y   IRAN

Antalya

Cyprus   SYRIA   IRAQ

Mediterranean LEBANON
Sea

ISRAEL JORD.

www.marco-polo.com

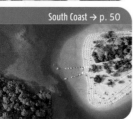
SYMBOLS

INSIDER TIP Insider Tip

★ Highlight

●●●● Best of ...

☆ Scenic view

☺ Responsible travel: fair
trade principles and the
environment respected

**PRICE CATEGORIES
HOTELS**

Expensive	over 175 lira
Moderate	65–175 lira
Budget	under 65 lira

The prices are for two persons
in a double room per night
including breakfast

**PRICE CATEGORIES
RESTAURANTS**

Expensive	over 65 lira
Moderate	15–65 lira
Budget	under 35 lira

The prices are for a three
course meal including drinks

On the cover: Surreal landscape p. 66 | The Hagia Sophia in Istanbul p. 42

CONTENTS

Central Anatolia → p. 62

South-east Anatolia → p. 72

Black Sea Coast → p. 80

Road atlas → p. 118
Zonguldak
İstanbul
K
Karabük
575
0-4
Kocaeli
650
Bursa
Eskişehir
200
Polatlı

DID YOU KNOW?

Timeline → p. 12
Local specialities → p. 26
A place in the sun → p. 38
Books & Films → p. 44
Budgeting → p. 107
Currency converter → p. 108
Weather in İzmir → p. 111

MAPS IN THE GUIDEBOOK

(120 A1) Page numbers and coordinates refer to the road atlas
(0) Site/address located off the map. Coordinates are also given for places that are not marked on the road atlas
(U A1) Refers to the street map of Istanbul inside the back cover

INSIDE BACK COVER:
PULL-OUT MAP →

PULL-OUT MAP 📖

(📖 A–B 2–3) Refers to the removable pull-out map
(📖 a–b 2–3) Refers to the additional inset maps on the pull-out map

The best MARCO POLO Insider Tips

Our top 15 Insider Tips

INSIDER TIP Sesame sensation

The best dessert to enjoy after fish is some delicious *sıcak halva* in one of Gümüşlük's restaurants on the Bodrum peninsula right at the sea (photo right) → p. 36

INSIDER TIP Pure nature

West of Marmaris are the two peninsulas of Reşadiye and Bozburun extend out into the Aegean: untouched landscapes far removed from mass tourism → p. 61

INSIDER TIP Fresh fish

The fresh trout eaten in front of the magnificent backdrop of Manavgat Waterfalls – halfway between Antalya and Alanya – tastes especially good → p. 53

INSIDER TIP Village with an underwater city

At the small, enchanted coastal village of Kaleköy you can dive to the ruins of a submerged Mediterranean city → p. 59

INSIDER TIP Hookah heaven

The beautiful, handmade hookahs that are traditionally sold at the Kemeraltı Bazaar in İzmir, display ornate craftsmanship and make for highly decorative souvenirs – even if you never want to use it → p. 46

INSIDER TIP Handmade pottery

If you would like to try your hand at making some earthenware pottery (not that easy), you can give it a whirl in the village of Avanos in Cappadocia – under expert guidance of course → p. 66

INSIDER TIP Horse riding at sunrise

Set out on horseback with the Rainbow Ranch in Göreme and you will feel like you are on another planet. Experienced and non-experienced riders alike can ride through Cappadocia's countryside with its extraordinary rock formations and surreal landscape of 'fairy chimneys'. → p. 67

BEST OF ...

FOR FREE

● *Home to colourful butterflies*
Right on the sea, and not far from Fethiye, is *Butterfly Valley*. Countless butterflies congregate here and the valley, with its beautiful beach, is a small piece of heaven. You can get there in comfort by boat or take a short hike → p. 58

● *A visit to the republic's founder*
In the heart of Ankara is the most famous mausoleum in the country: *Anıt Kabir*, the tomb of the republic's founder Mustafa Kemal Atatürk. The neo-classical monument is the 'place of pilgrimage' for the Turkish Republic; admission is free → p. 64

● *The oldest city in the world*
When British archaeologists discovered *Çatalhöyük* last century, they gradually uncovered a settled urban area that existed at least 7000 years ago – a wonderful open air museum! → p. 71

● *The Big Blue*
Mosques are one of the attractions that don't charge an entrance fee and one of the most beautiful mosques in Turkey is the *Blue Mosque* in Istanbul. In the same line of sight as the Hagia Sophia it represents the blossoming of the Ottoman Empire (photo) → p. 42

● *The enchanted palace*
In the far east of the country, on a hill, from where you can see Mount Ararat and the border to Iran, there is an enchanted *palace* that was built for Prince Ishak Pascha. A magical place that you can see for a small donation → p. 79

● *Abraham's cave*
There is no admission fee to see *Abraham's birthplace* in Şanlıurfa. The founding father of the Jews, Christians and Muslims was said to have been born here and it is a place of pilgrimage for the followers of the three 'religions of the book' → p. 76

● ● ● ● Dots in guidebook refer to 'Best of ...' tips

● *Traditional shopping*

The district with the covered market streets, the bazaar, is an import from the Orient and visiting a bazaar is an experience in itself. You will find a market district in almost every big city in Anatolia but the bazaar in Istanbul, which was built in 1461, is considered the largest in the world → **p. 42**

● *Promenade*

Turkey has miles of coastline and count-less number of cities on the sea. Every one of them has a promenade *(piyasa caddesi)*, where people walk in the even-ing whilst snacking on sunflower seeds – one of the most beautiful promenades is in İzmir (photo) → **p. 46**

● *Picnic*

You only need a small area of lawn to set up a barbecue and enjoy one of the country's favourite leisure activities, the picnic. There are even restaurants that offer a barbecue where you can grill the meat yourself – such as the beach restaurant *Maymi* in Marmaris → **p. 60**

● *Fish in Fethiye*

In Turkey going out for a meal of some fresh fish is all about the con-versations with friends over a bottle of raki. In the nationally famous fish restaurant *Rafet* on the waterfront promenade in Fethiye you will get to know the rules of a raki evening → **p. 57**

● *Cold smoke*

The hookah *(nargile)* was until recently almost a thing of the past but it is currently undergoing a renaissance in Turkey. The tobacco comes in various flavours and is passed through cooling water before you inhale it. You can indulge in this vice in the historic setting of the courtyard of *Cevahir Konukevi* in Şanlıurfa → **p. 76**

● *Journey through time*

In Turkey there are 131 ancient cities and countless more that are wait-ing to be discovered and excavated. The ancient Greek city of *Ephesus* near İzmir has been excavated and partially reconstructed – a highlight of any trip to Turkey! → **p. 48**

ONLY IN

BEST OF ...

● *Medusa head*
When it rains in Istanbul there are surprising discoveries to be made below ground. *Yerebatan* is a Byzantine cistern where a Medusa heads might send shivers down your spine → p. 43

● *Greek highlights*
There are numerous archaeological museums in Turkey, but the *museum in Antalya* offers some of the greatest highlights due to the many Greek archaeological sites in the area → p. 54

● *Underwater show*
The only *Museum of Underwater Archaeology* in Turkey offers an entertaining show in the basement of The Bodrum Castle of The Knights of St John with fascinating displays of finds from the sea (photo) → p. 34

● *Old Orient*
The *old Şanlıurfa bazaar* is completely under cover and is the most Oriental place in Turkey. No amount of rain can ruin your shopping spree through its narrow streets filled with vendors selling carpets and copperware → p. 76

● *Caravanserai*
Just like they did 500 years ago, today you too can escape to a *caravanserai* when the weather turns bad in Diyarbakır. The restored building has a restaurant and bar, sometimes musicians also perform folk music from their region → p. 74

● *Citadel on the hill*
The city fathers of Ankara put in a lot of effort into restoring the old castle and today the attractive buildings have found new life as restaurants and other cultural facilities. A worthwhile detour in bad weather → p. 65

RAIN

RELAX AND CHILL OUT
Take it easy and spoil yourself

● *Feel as good as new*

The traditional place of relaxation is the hammam, a Turkish bath. After hours of sweating, washing and massage, you will leave the hammam a new person. The Ottoman baths in Istanbul are beautiful and a good example is the one behind the Süleymaniye Mosque (photo) → p. 44

● *A bathing holiday far from the sea*

The famous thermal baths of Bursa in southern Istanbul (photo) are devoted entirely to relaxation. Their fame dates back to ancient times but today there are numerous hotels that offer thermal spas, such as the *Çelik Palas* → p. 38

● *In the cotton castle*

The *Pamukkale travertine terraces* are spectacular so take the unique opportunity to bathe in warm waters under open skies in one of the white terrace pools of the Turkish 'cotton castle' → p. 49

● *Solitude in the clouds*

The Ayder Plateau, above the Black Sea, seems to be as high as the clouds and this pristine natural paradise is the ideal place to enjoy some solitude at *Berghof Liligum* → p. 86

● *Mud wrap*

The *hot springs at the Köyceğiz Lake* are the ideal excuse to wallow in some mud! The mud is thought to have healing properties, which is why you will see people encrusted in black mud but looking happy and radiant. You can reach them by boat from Dalyan → p. 61

● *Other-worldly*

If you are looking to relax in the peace and quiet of nature, you should wait until the season ends, in autumn, and book yourself in at *Kale Pansiyon* in Kekova. The village is accessible by water only and is idyllically situated near Kaş. A special and other-worldly place! → p. 59

INTRODUCTION

DISCOVER TURKEY!

It is an interesting fact that tulips don't come from the Netherlands, but from Turkey and that the Garden of Eden was apparently located in south-eastern Anatolia. One of the oldest known human settlements is situated in the Central Anatolian Çatalhöyük, it dates back to 7 BC, making it as old as Jericho. And it was apparently the early inhabitants of Anatolia that were the first to start writing almost 4000 years ago. Who would have guessed?

Come to Turkey and surprise yourself! In hardly any other European holiday destination will visitors experience such a myriad of contrasts: geographical, social, historical and political. Geographically, Turkey lies between Western Europe and East Asia with the Bosporus River forming the border. A trip along the west-east axis of the country leads from Thrace's cornfields, on the European side, across the picturesque bays of

Photo: Mediterranean coast in Kemer

Open to the public: the Mevlana Museum in Konya was a lodge for the order of the whirling dervishes

the Aegean coast, past the snow-covered mountain ranges of the Anatolian Plateau, through fertile valleys up to the volcanic Kurdistan Alps on the eastern border. From the north to the south the landscape goes from the wooded slopes of the Pontiac Taurus Mountains, at the Black Sea, to the enormous Anatolian steppe, and the lunar landscape of Cappadocia, bounded by the Taurus Mountains, before reaching the shores of the southern Mediterranean coast. Anatolia has been shaped for thousands of years by the people (and religions) moving between the East and the West – on their way through Turkey they often used the same routes as the crusaders or the caravans on the Silk Route. Hittites, Greeks, Romans, Byzantines, Seljuk Turks, Mongols, crusaders and the Ottomans have all left marks that are still visible up to this day in Anatolia.

Turkey has something to offer everyone: for the beach lover there is 1500km/932mi of the Aegean and Mediterranean coastline with secluded bays and the cleanest

water in southern Europe. Nature lovers will discover a wonderful variety of flora and fauna and some of the last specimens of the Caretta sea turtles hatch on some of the Mediterranean beaches. There are also lots of options for outdoor enthusiasts and sports lovers. For hikers there are

Antiquity and early Christianity

hills and high mountain ranges, for winter sports enthusiasts there are a growing number of ski resorts and for divers there is the shimmering underwater world off the Mediterranean coast. For those interested in history the whole country is one large open air museum. Even Greece does not have as many Greek antiquites as there are in Asia Minor which include the churches, palaces and castles of the Byzantine emperors (4th–15th century), the magnificent buildings from the Islamic Ottoman era (16th–19th century), the wonderful mosques of the court architect, Sinan, in Istanbul and Edirne and the medresses (religious schools) of Konya. Besides Israel, there is no country that has as many destinations for Christian pilgrims and is as theologically interesting as Turkey is. It is believed that it was in Antakya (Antioch) on the Syrian border that the disciples of Jesus called themselves 'Christians' and where Paul's missionary journey began. Mary and the Apostle John are said to have died in Ephesus. The early Christian congregations hid from the Romans in the caves of Cappadocia.

Today 70 million Turks are proud to be self-sufficient and the produce that you see at the weekly markets comes mostly from their own fields and farms. Nevertheless, the farmers are still the poorest members of society. Three quarters of them don't

1683–1923 Decline of the Ottoman Empire	1876 First Constitution	1914–18 World War I; the Ottomans side with the Germans	1919 Turkish War of Independence led by Mustafa Kemal Pascha against the partitioning of Turkey	1922–38 Kemalist cultural revolution	29 October 1923 Founding of the Turkish Republic

own their own land and work for large-scale landowners. Industrial production has made a huge leap in the past few years. Whether electronics, household appliances, computers, motor vehicles (produced under licence from Japan and Germany) or men's fashion – the label 'Made in Turkey' is no longer ridiculed. On the contrary, in recent years Turkey – with its 7 per cent annual growth rate – has by far been the most dynamic economy in Europe. This has not, however, led to equitable levels of income distribution and falling un-employment figures and the gulf between rich and poor in Turkey is larger than the EU average.

City on the upswing: boom town Istanbul

In particular, the area that makes up greater Istanbul is booming in a way that is unparalleled in Europe. The city's 15 million inhabitants increases by 100,000 every year, with a new skyscraper built almost every month. Istanbul is also set to become a banking centre serving the area between the Balkans and the Persian Gulf. However, the development of Istanbul also contributes to the ever-increasing gap between the wealthy in the west and the poor in the east of Turkey. Besides individual Anatolian beacons of industry such as Gaziantep, Kayseri, Mersin and Konya, there has been no move towards developing the Kurdish settlements in the south-east of Turkey. The constant conflict with the Kurdish minority has not been solved, so much so that the armed struggle flares up regularly, which discourages investors despite the fact that the state offers large tax rebates.

Whilst the average income of the upper class in the cities in the west of Turkey are almost on par with those in central Europe, poverty is rife in the eastern part of the country and the outskirts of the cities nationwide. Poverty causes many people cling on to an old, partly archaic value system that includes a strict patriarchy, a belief in the concept of honour (that does not stop at honour killing), and a way of thinking that is focused around clan structures. This sector of society is in stark contrast to the urban middle class, who feel closer to the inhabitants of London or Paris than they do to the villagers in eastern Anatolia. Since the end of the 1990s the younger generation in the cities developed their own dynamics; they have ensured that their country keeps a connection to Europe. In Istanbul you can live as if in London, Berlin or Rome, with a cosmopolitan and educated middle class choosing to socialise and

1952
NATO membership

1960/1971/1980
Military coups

1974
Turkish invasion of Northern Cyprus

2002
The moderate Islamist AKP sweeps to power

2005
Start of membership negotiations with the EU; full membership is the goal

2009
Turkey survives the global financial crisis relatively unscathed

meet up in the pubs. They have been the vehicle for the reforms that paved the way for Turkey to become a member of the EU.

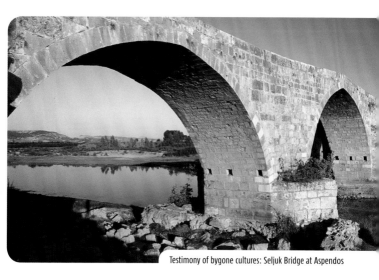

Testimony of bygone cultures: Seljuk Bridge at Aspendos

But now, this alignment is in question. The economic gap and the resulting differences in value systems is an ideological conflict which divides the country. Until the end of the 1990s Turkey was dominated by the spirit of Kemalism, a doctrine that goes back to the founding father Kemal Atatürk and which sees a radical modernisation that bypasses Islam and focuses more on the West and includes the separation of the state and religion. However, since 2002 the country has been led by a conservative-Islamic government, that a lot of the certainties of Kemalism, one that is trying to align itself to the traditions of the old Ottoman Empire. The resulting resurgence of Islam has led to a kind of 'culture war', which is evident in almost all areas of life, not only in the dispute over the wearing of headscarves or the prohibition of alcohol, but

At the crossroads: a country in transition

in the strengthening of traditional ideas as a whole. Although the government officially holds on to their EU alignment, Europe is now no longer the measure of all things. Turkey is once again looking to the East and the Arab region for partners and with their growing economic success their eagerness to follow the rules and regulations from Brussels is on the wane. Turkey is therefore developing, in a very conflict-laden process, a synthesis between the East and the West, which reflects its geographical location.

Get ready to lose some of your preconceived ideas or prejudices about Turkey on your journey through the country and allow yourself to be surprised! Discover Turkey!

WHAT'S HOT

1 East meets West

Fashion His Turkish homeland is always present in Atil Kutoğlus' designs, which have had worldwide success *(Bostan Sok. 9/2, Istanbul, photo)*. The balancing act between the Orient and the Occident is represented in the creations of Erol Albayrak, a fashion designer known for his colourful designs *(Prof Dr Orhan Ersek Sok. Güçer Apt. 45/1, Istanbul)*. While Iana Makridis is still waiting for her big breakthrough, it may only be a matter of time for this fashion designer *(www.ianamakridis.com)*.

On the streets

Culinary Sample something on the roadside. On the street food tour Banu Ozden, from the Culinary Institute in Istanbul, leads you from stall to stall. On the menu is grilled fish, *köfte* (small Turkish meatballs) or dumplings called *mantı (www.istanbulculinary.com/eng/)*. Tucked away in the little back streets of Beyoğlu are some small eateries and markets. Annie Pertain shows you where to go *(www.turkishflavours.com, photo)*. Whether you prefer a wine-tasting tour through Cappadocia or a meal with the locals – *Spoontrip* organises your culinary adventures for you *(www.spoontrip.com)*.

Guaranteed style

Designer It is not the intimate boutique hotels that everyone is talking about, but the large designer hotels around Antalya. The *Hillside Su* is all done out in futuristic white with only the façade showing some colour *(Dumlupınar Bulvarı, Konyaaltı Koruluğu Yanı)*. Also colourful is the exterior of *Adam & Eve* and you will certainly not forget its large pool that overlooks the sea *(Iskele Mevkii, photo)*. Design is also held in high regard in Istanbul. The *Lush Hip Hotel* boasts 35 individually styled rooms *(Sıraselviler Cad. 12)*.

By the book

Tünel Turkish authors have celebrated success in Europe in recent years and have thus enthused the general public. Cafés now include a reading corner, where newspapers from around the world are are on offer, and the patrons enjoy passionate discussions about the literary scene. This trend is most pronounced in Istanbul's Tünel district. Intellectuals meet at the *Ada* where those who don't have their noses in books, spend their time people watching *(İstiklal Cad. 445, www.adakitapcafe.com, photo)*. Perhaps Yeşim Ağaoğlu was once inspired here? Her poems have Istanbul as a recurring theme *(yesimpoetry.blogspot.com)* and while on the subject, why not pay a visit to the *Divan Literary Museum*? *(Galip Dede Cad. 15)*.

Horseback trekking

Giddyup The perfect escort for a hike through the Turkish landscape is a four legged one and horseback trekking is an adventure not only for animal lovers. With your draft horse you will trek through parts of the Taurus Mountains with its rugged cliffs, snow-covered peaks and green forests *(www.time outdoor.de/Default.aspx?tabid=110, photo)*. With *Kirkit* it takes seven days on horseback through Anatolia but half day tours in Cappadocia are also available *(Amiral Tafdil Sok. 12, Istanbul, www.kirkit.com)*.

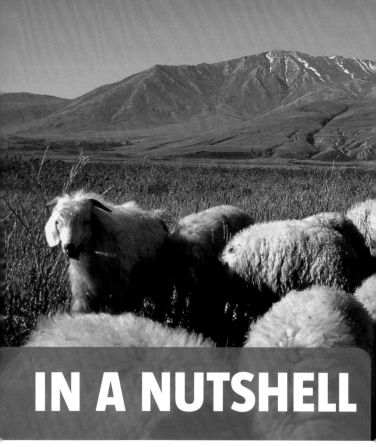

IN A NUTSHELL

ATATÜRK

Turkey's founder, Mustafa Kemal Atatürk, is revered because he saved the country from partitioning and founded the Republic, a nation with a new perspective. During World War I the Sultan was allied with the Germans. Once the war was over the victors wanted the country divided amongst Italy, France, the United Kingdom, Greece and Armenia. Only a small part of the Anatolian heartland was to remain under Turkish control. On the Black Sea coast a group of young Turkish officers, under the leadership of Mustafa Kemal, organised a resistance to the Sultanate and the partitioning of their country. What began as a guerrilla war became a national resistance movement. The goal: the foundation of the state of 'Turkey'.

After regaining state sovereignty the Turkish Republic was formally founded on 29 October 1923, Mustafa Kemal began as President (he received the honorary name Atatürk in 1934, '*Ata*' means 'father' or 'ancestor') with the second part of his ambitious revolution: the radical transformation of the country from within. He abolished the Sultanate in 1922 and then the Caliphate in 1924 and with this the dynasty of the Ottoman Empire – which held both these offices – was at its end. Atatürk then dissolved the Islamic orders,

Photo: Shepherd in eastern Anatolia

Turkish society changed rapidly: here are some fundamental points and background information for a clearer understanding

prohibited religious schools and the wearing of veils in public buildings and gave women equal rights. In 1930 they were allowed the vote – before some western European countries. Atatürk introduced a civil law code based on the Swiss model and a criminal code based on the Italian model. A drastic turning point was the replacement of the Arabic script with the Latin alphabet. Atatürk died in 1938 in the Istanbul Dolmabahçe Palace at the age of 57 years from liver cirrhosis. His impressive mausoleum is in Ankara (Anıt Kabir).

CHRISTIANS

Christians in Turkey today are only a small minority. However, the situation was different under the Ottoman Empire when, at the beginning of the 20th century, there were several million Christians. Their numbers declined considerably when the Armenians were expelled during World War I and a large population exchange took place between Greece and Turkey after the Turkish war of independence ended in 1923. Today almost all Greek and Armenian Christians live in Istanbul. There is an ever-shrinking group of Syriac Orthodox Christians in the Kurdish areas along the Syrian border. In contrast, the number of Protestants and Catholics living in the big cities like Istanbul and İzmir or at the Mediterranean is growing.

If there is talk about the difficult situation of Christians in Turkey, then it usually has to do with the rights of the long established Greek and Armenian communities. Their status is regulated in the Treaty of Lausanne, where minority rights, such as having their own schools and other cultural institutions, are formalised. There were conflicts (and they are ongoing) regarding church property – some of which have been arbitrarily seized – and regarding the autonomous training of clerics. The most important priest seminary of the Orthodox Greeks was closed over thirty years ago, in part because the community does not want to place its institution under the Turkish Ministry of Education. In the wake of becoming a member of the EU, the Turkish government has been forced to give the church a better legal status and grant greater organisational freedom. Some improvements are evident since 2005 and in 2010 congregations were first allowed to celebrate in symbolic places like the Sümela Monastery in Trabzon or the Ahtamar Church at Lake Van.

EARTHQUAKES
Turkey is an earthquake zone and the north is considered to have one of the highest risks of earthquakes in the world. The North Anatolian Fault expands from the east at Erzurum to the Gulf of Saros at the Greek border. The biggest catastrophe in 100 years took place in August and November 1999 in western Turkey. More than 18,000 people died. The severe earthquake was particularly threatening to the metropolis Istanbul, because its epicentre was less than 100km/62mi from the city. In October 2011 a heavy tremor claimed a few hundred victims in the cities of Van and Ercis at Lake Van.

FAMILY PROTECTION
Often you will see the sign 'Aile Çay Bahçesi' (family tea garden) or 'Aile Salonu' (family salon) at the entrance which tells you that bachelors are separated from men with families or couples. This is no longer seen in big city cafés and restaurants but is still valid in simpler eateries in the country. This is meant to protect the women from tiresome male onlookers – which often occurs, especially if the men have had one too many drinks.

FLORA & FAUNA
The flora and fauna is as diverse and as varied as the regions of the country. All species that appear in central Europe and the Balkans are also found in Turkey. In the more remote regions there are still wolves, jackals and bears. In southern Turkey there are various tortoise and lizard species but sadly, the last Turkish leopard was killed in 1979. There is also an impressive variety of bird species that you can see near the lakes. Cormorants, pelicans, herons and storks (especially white storks) visit in the summer and in autumn they move in beautiful formations to the south.

FOOTBALL
Football is the most popular sport in Turkey by far; the love affair with the game starts in childhood – playing in the street –

and extends to a lifelong enthusiasm for one of the major professional clubs. Until a few years ago the three biggest clubs in Istanbul *Fenerbahçe, Galatasaray* and *Beşiktaş* were the dominating triumvirate of the league and regularly decided the championship between them. But in recent years some Anatolian clubs like *Trabzonspor* or *Bursaspor* have become serious opponents and have weakened the dominance of the big three. Turkish football is now a bit more varied and the enthusiasm is even more widespread. The only bitter pill for fans to swallow is that the national team remains weak at the big international tournaments. The women are not just fans: the Turkish women's football league began in 2005 with seven teams; in 2010 they had 1500 players in 72 clubs.

HAMMAM

Warm, splashing water in marble basins, hot steam under high vaulted domes: the Turkish bath is a must for tourists. Women and men are usually separated in the hammams but in some tourist baths men and women are allowed to mix. You will find a hammam in every city.

ISLAM

Officially, 99 per cent of the Turkish population are Muslims, the majority of which are Sunni. The Holy Book – the Koran – contains the revelations of the Prophet Mohammed in verse form and it must be in the original Arabic to be called the Koran. For scholars of private Koranic schools it is considered a considerable challenge to memorise the entire text. In government schools only general religion is taught; Christians and Jews have their own schools. There are about a quarter of Muslims that belong to the Alevi sect. They are followers of Ali, a son-in-law of Mohammed.

Minaret in Kalkan

The two main Moslem festivals are *Kurban* (The Feast of the Sacrifice) and *Ramazan bayramı* (Sugar Feast). At the Feast of the Sacrifice those who can afford it sacrifice a young sheep or calf in commemoration of the sacrifice Abraham was willing to make. According to Jewish and Muslim rites the sacrifice is done without anaesthesia so that the blood will run freely from the animal. The meat is then kosher (Jewish) or halal (Islamic). Two thirds of the meat is distributed to the poor or those in need. During Ramadan, the Muslim month of fasting, the majority of Muslims refrain from eating, drinking and smoking between sunrise and sunset. It is difficult to find an open restaurant in the province at this time.

Market women at the Manavgat vegetable market in Side

KURDS

The Kurds (today about 8 per cent of the Turkish population) once lived in the south-eastern provinces, but many have moved to the big western cities in the past decades in search of work. In Istanbul alone there are at least 3 million people of Kurdish decent. The Kurds are not – unlike the Armenians or the Greek – recognised as an official minority and have faced the pressure of assimilation for a long time. These days the government deals more calmly with them as a cultural minority but if anyone goes as far as calling for Kurdish autonomy, they can face charges of separatism and face a prison sentence.

LANGUAGE

The Turkish spoken in Turkey is one of the Central Asian Oghuz languages of the Ural-Altai group. During the Ottoman period many Persian and Arabic elements were included and in the 1920s French expressions such as *şoför* (chauffeur) or *asansör* (elevator) were added. Communication amongst the different Turkish people is difficult but not impossible one example are the Azeri (Azerbaijan Turks), who speak a strong Turkish dialect making communication easy. As a visitor in the country's tourist areas and in the major cities you can communicate quite well in English.

MUSIC

Whether it is Shakira, Tarkan, Turkish 'art music' or Sufi sounds: music will accompany you wherever you go in Turkey. Although a lot of pop music is played, Turkish music offers a wide regional and tonal variety. The 'art music' (*Türk*

Sanat Müziği) with Byzantine and Arabic influences requires a lot of voice discipline from the singers. The simple folk music of Anatolia and the Black Sea area sounds lively in comparison and does not need an orchestra. A few fiddles, drums and a *saz* (string instrument) are sufficient. You can get CDs relatively cheaply at good music stores (e.g. the D&R chain). Good Turkish pop can be found under the *Doublemoon* label, good ethno-sounds under *Kalan Müzik*.

OTTOMAN EMPIRE

The name comes from the dynasty's founder Osman (ruled 1288–1324), the dynasty's rule lasted until 1922. A total of 37 sultans ruled the Empire, some only ruled for a few months, before they became victims of an intrigue or fratricide. After Mehmed II conquered Constantinople (known as *Fatih,* the conqueror, by the Turks), the sultans ruled, from the Balkan to Algeria, for centuries. Its downfall began in the 19th century, ending in World War I and the foundation of the modern Republic. Despite attempts by the new government to wipe out all memories of the old empire, today anything Ottoman is undergoing a slightly kitsch revival in art and culture. The Ottoman elements are woven into the Turkish culture today are no longer considered objectionable.

POLITICAL SYSTEM

According to the constitution, Turkey is a Western style parliamentary democracy – the only one in the Muslim world. Members of the Grand National Assembly of Turkey in Ankara and the mayors of towns and cities are elected every four years in a secret ballot by eligible voters over 18 years. Many reform packages, with increased freedom of expression and limiting the power of the army, have been adopted since 2001.

WOMEN

Women enjoy equal legal rights in Turkey where women were given the right to vote in 1930 (see the section 'Atatürk') and the schools have been co-educational since 1925. Participation of women in public life is the social norm in Turkey: at universities the women make up 50 per cent. Nevertheless, Turkish women's rights activists are fighting for more rights, such as gender quotas in parliament. However, conservative Islamic parties and organisations that have gained influence in recent years are opposed to these proposals. The number of so-called 'honour killings' has increased, mostly in the Kurdish community. The rapid social change has not yet reached the conservative rural communities and women in rural areas are still suppressed by their husbands.

FOOD & DRINK

The culinary diversity of Turkish cuisine is on par with any other Mediterranean country and enjoyable for tourists as it is delicious and not overly spiced. The origin of many Turkish dishes can be traced back to the nomadic period of the early Turkish people, such as the various types of breads baked in clay ovens and the yoghurt or lamb dishes.

These traditions later merged with the cuisine from Asia Minor's coastal cultures, especially their way of preparing fish. During the Ottoman era European and North African influences were also included. There are even recipes that have been around since the Roman era. A character-

istic of Turkish cuisine is that the preparation is complex and time consuming, even for those dishes that seem to be quite simple. Anyone who has ever watched a Turkish housewife prepare *dolma* – stuffed cabbage or vine leaves – will realise that the Turks take a lot of time in the evenings for the main course whether in a private family home or in a *lokanta* or restaurant. Breakfast, on the other hand, is less substantial: some white bread with feta cheese, olives and jam. At lunchtime it is usually a soup and a light vegetable dish.

In the tourist areas on the Mediterranean coast traditional cuisine has taken the back seat in favour of more standard in-

Photo: Meatballs *(köfte)* and marinated vegetables

More than just *döner* and kebabs – a Turkish dinner is a treat for the eyes and the palate. The main ingredient: plenty of time

ternational fare. The rich buffets served in the holiday villages caters to every taste and vegetarians also get their money's worth as salads and vegetable dishes are an integral part of Turkish menus. Many restaurants cater specially for vegetarian customers. For some the cold starters *(meze)* are the highlight of Turkish cuisine. The starters include vegetables of all kinds (usually marinated in olive oil) crabs, mus-

sels, calamari, *humus* (puréed chickpeas), seasonal salads and puff pastry pies. No restaurant would serve their *meze* without *rakı* (a strong grape spirit flavoured with anise) which also goes very well with creamy feta and honeydew melon.

The Turkish expect a dish to taste of the main ingredient and not to be overpowered by sauces or covered in spices. Lamb and beef are usually grilled on a skewer

LOCAL SPECIALITIES

▶ **acı** – pastry made from very hot red peppers

▶ **ahtapot salatası** – calamari rings in oil with green olives

▶ **arnavut ciğeri** – cubes of liver tossed in spiced flour and pan fried (eaten cold)

▶ **baklava** – sweet dish with layers of gossamer thin filo pastry filled with pistachios or walnuts – often very sweet (photo right)

▶ **balık ızgara** – grilled fish served in several variations

▶ **biber dolması** – peppers filled with minced meat and rice (photo left)

▶ **bugulama** – fish stewed in its own juices with onions and potatoes

▶ **çiğ köfte** – hotly spiced raw meat balls: the only dish that Turkish men prepare themselves

▶ **halva** – 'Turkish honey', popular dessert often eaten after fish

▶ **iç pilav** – rice dish with raisins, liver and peas

▶ **işkembe corbası** – tripe soup which is preferably enjoyed in the early morning after a long night out

▶ **iskender kebap** – slices of *döner* on flat bread with yoghurt, doused over with melted butter

▶ **karnı yarık** – aubergines filled with onions and minced meat (eaten warm)

▶ **kaymaklı cevizli muz** – dessert of banana slices with walnuts and home-made cream

▶ **köfte** – a national dish of small well seasoned meatballs, either grilled or pan fried

▶ **kuzu pirzola** – tender lamb chops that are either grilled (*izgara*) or fried (*tava*)

▶ **kuzu tandır** – leg of lamb, oven roasted

▶ **mantı** – a kind of ravioli which is served with garlic yoghurt and fresh mint

▶ **muhallebi** – milk based pudding thickened with rice flour and rice

▶ **patlıcan salatası** – salad made of feta cheese and charcoal grilled aubergines

▶ **roca salatası** – rocket salad

▶ **sigara böreği** – puff pastry rolls, traditionally filled with feta cheese and parsley

▶ **şiş kebap** – pieces of lamb, grilled with tomatoes, onions and peppers

(*şiş*), sparingly seasoned and served almost always without a sauce. The meat is usually accompanied by a salad and rice, bulgur or potatoes. Besides the 'fast food' option of thin slices of *döner* on bread (*pide*) there are dozens of other ways that

Cheap and delicious: *döner* kebab

meat is prepared. The variations *patlıcan kebabı* (aubergines filled with mince meat on a skewer) or *saç kebabı* (lamb cut in strips with mushrooms and tomatoes, fried in a pan) come from east Anatolia. Poultry is often prepared in the oven. In coastal towns fish and seafood naturally dominate the menu. Highly recommended are *fenerbalığı* (monkfish), *levrek* (sea bass), *lüfer* (blue perch), *kalkanbalığı* (turbot) and *palamut* (tuna). You can also get fresh lobster (*istakoz*) on the Mediterranean coast. The locals on the north coast apparently know more than 40 ways of preparing the famous Black Sea sardines *(hamsi)*.

Turkish dessert also holds a few surprises and includes a variety of puff pastries, pies covered in syrup and chocolate puddings and there are also lots of succulent fruits: honeydew and watermelons, grapes, peaches and sometimes also black mulberries *(karadut)*. It is rounded off with a cup of strong Turkish mocha *(türk kahvesi)* ordered either *sade* (unsweetened), *orta* (semi-sweet) or *şekerli* (sweetened).

Turkey's national drink is tea *(çay)* and it is served in small, tulip-shaped glasses and sweetened to taste. When you start to drink at least five cups of tea a day – that is when you know that you have embraced Turkey! Nowadays instant coffee is also consumed, and international coffee house franchises are very popular. Still water is called *su*, sparkling water is *soda* and the refreshing *ayran* is a mix of water and yoghurt. Foreign wines are generally only available in exclusive restaurants but the local brands *Doluca* or *Kavaklıdere* are good table wines. When it comes to beer, the best is *Efes.* Alcohol is not served everywhere, especially not in the strongly Muslim cities in central and eastern Anatolia.

There are distinctions between restaurants (*restoran, lokanta*) and simple eateries (*meyhane*), while *birahane* are pubs that are best avoided by women. Typically, in a good restaurant there will be a host of waiters ready to serve you. In eateries called *ocakbaşı* you can have food *(ızgara)* that is prepared on a large grill *(mangal)* in the middle of the room, a tasty meal that will be easy on the pocket too. In *pastahane* (patisseries) there are often also cake and tarts.

If you enjoy a meal and the service is good, you generally leave a ten per cent tip.

SHOPPING

Bargaining for an item in a retail store is just as uncommon here as it is at home as the prices are fixed. However, bazaar traders and souvenir shop owners are usually prepared to bargain, but it is not the done thing to bargain someone down for an item you are not genuinely interested in buying. And another tip: don't name a price first and your offer should never be lower than 30–40 per cent of what the trader suggested. Sometimes the owner will offer you a cup of tea. Have the courage to bargain, be firm but always remain friendly in your dealings. In the more modern shops in the big cities the prices are as marked and not negotiable.

ANTIQUES

Some of the most popular souvenirs to take back from Turkey include copper and brassware, hookahs, silver and gold jewellery, ceramics and antiques. Antiques are understood to be pieces that are more than a hundred years old. As a rule, taking antiques out of the country is only possible when they are accompanied by official documentation. In the past this seemed too complicated tourists – after all, you don't even need to dig to find old stones and coins in Turkey. However, since the case of a foreign holidaymaker – sentenced to six weeks for having a nondescript stone and released only after paying a 6000 euro fine – the temptation to 'steal' debris has passed. It is not uncommon that, after closer inspection, the newly acquired 'antique' turns out to be a forgery. Fake antiquities are often found among the 'ancient' coins, which are sold around the archaeological sites.

CARPETS

Hand-woven carpets are still being made on countless looms and the best come from Bergama, Konya, Kayseri and Uşak. When buying a carpet, there are a few things to look out for. The first is the more knots the carpet has, the more valuable it is. As proof of quality workmanship, the patterns on the back of the carpet should be just as even as those on the front. Natural silk is more valuable than artificial silk; cotton is more valuable than synthetic fibres. Test whether synthetic fibres have been mixed

Carpets, leather and antiques: if you want to haggle in a Turkish bazaar you will need patience and a sense of humour

in by pulling out a few threads and lighting them with a match, the smell will be your indicator. If the pattern changes in colour a lot, it gives you an indication of the degrees of difficulty in the carpet's production. When assessing the price it is worth bearing in mind that 10ft² of high-quality carpet takes about 100 days of weaving!

GOLD & SILVER

When it comes to gold jewellery, the same principle applies in Turkey as everywhere else: the more work has been done on a piece of jewellery, the more expensive it is. It is definitely worth seeking out jewellers who are well away from the well-beaten tourist path. Reputable jewellers will have a notice up with the day's current gold price and you should definitely request a certificate of authenticity! Although the gold price has also increased in Turkey

since the global financial crisis in 2009/10, it is still cheaper than elsewhere in Europe. Silver is also reasonably priced – always check for the stamp on the inside or on the back of the piece of jewellery.

LEATHER & COTTON

Products made of leather and cotton are also among the classic Turkish souvenirs, but you won't get first class products everywhere. The leather should not be stained and should be dyed well and it should not be thick and stiff as you will want your trousers or jacket to fit like second skin. There should also be a leather quality label which will ensure that you are not buying defective goods. You can also purchase cotton items at most markets at reasonable prices. The cottons are often dyed naturally and decorated with beautiful embroidery.

THE PERFECT ROUTE

THE QUEEN OF THE CITIES

Every roundtrip through Turkey begins and ends in the 3000 year old metropolis of two world empires, in ① *Istanbul* → p. 41, previously Constantinople, once Byzantium. The lively and booming metropolis on the Bosporus is a world in its own and is alone worth a trip. From Istanbul you first head for green ② *Bursa* → p. 36. It lies at the foot of the 2500m/8202ft high Uludağ and is the birthplace of the Ottoman Empire. Here the sultans erected their first capital city and it was from Bursa that the conquests of the Balkan and Constantinople were launched.

RESORTS AND TERRACED HOT SPRINGS

Past ③ *İzmir* → p. 45, one of the most important ports in the country, you then reach ④ *Bodrum* → p. 32. When the Turkish dream of taking a break from the tedium of everyday life and enjoying some time at the seaside, they think of the 'white town by the sea' and Bodrum is the perfect retreat, even if it does become a hectic tourist metropolis – at least in the summer. North-east of Bodrum, not far from the provincial town of Denizli, are the gleaming white travertine terraces of ⑤ *Pamukkale* → p. 49. The sight is intoxicating, and a dip in the hot springs is good for both body and soul.

WHIRLING DERVISHES AND 'FAIRY CHIMNEYS'

Further east, in the middle of Turkey, is ⑥ *Konya* → p. 68, the country's spiritual centre. The Sufi Mevlevi Order had its headquarters here, and the tomb of the whirling dervishes is still the city's focal point (photo left). The next stop on the way from the west to the east is ⑦ *Cappadocia* → p. 66. The volcanic landscape, near Nevşehir, seems like a landscape from another world. The strange soft volcanic rock 'fairy chimney' cones were formed by the wind and weather. The landscape harbours mysterious caves which served as a refuge for early Christians fleeing Roman persecution about 2000 years ago.

MYSTERIOUS ARABIA

In the south-east, on the border with Syria, is ⑧ *Şanlıurfa (Urfa)* → p. 75, a city whose Arabic roots are still alive today. Urfa is old –

Experience all of the fascinating facets of Turkey in a round trip: from the sea to the mountains, from Istanbul to Anatolia

so old that Abraham is said to have lived here – and Urfa's bazaar is the country's oldest and most mysterious shopping paradise in the country. **9** *Diyarbakır* → p. 74 is the unofficial capital of the Kurds in Turkey and is the most easterly point on the route. There is a lot of evidence of the conflict of the last few decades, but also of the pioneering spirit of its inhabitants. Diyarbakır is on the way to becoming a modern metropolis.

ATATÜRK'S CITY

From the Kurdish 'capital' city of the east the tour takes a big leap back to the west, to the country's official capital city. **10** *Ankara* → p. 63 is the city of Atatürk, the city of the Republic and the centre of modern Turkey. From the parliament to the presidential palace to Kemal Atatürk's mausoleum (photo left), this is where the centres and symbols of power are based.

PEARLS OF THE BLACK SEA

Still largely undiscovered by mass tourism, the 'pearls of the Black Sea' are located north-west of Ankara: **11** *Safranbolu* → p. 82 in the hinterland and **12** *Amasra* → p. 83 on the coast. Quite different from the tourist south, here you will discover the most beautiful classical houses in Turkey, and in Amasra the most scenic seaside resort of the Turkish Black Sea coast. From here the route goes via Zonguldak back to Istanbul.

About 3000km/1864mi. Recommended travel time: 14 days. Detailed map of the route on the back cover, in the road atlas and the pull-out map

WEST COAST

The western Aegean coast is a magical world of ancient ruins and beautiful beaches. From Istanbul to Bodrum there is a 700km/435mi long coast full of bays and coves. In the hinterland there are rolling hills where – thanks to the mild Mediterranean climate – olives, vineyards and tobacco thrive.

This area, which has been settled for more than 5000 years, offers magnificent remains from antiquity; Troy, Ephesus and Pergamum are just a few of the countless excavation and sightseeing sites. Impressive natural phenomena, such as the terraces of Pamukkale, alternate with marinas, holiday resorts and small fishing villages.

BODRUM

(128 C4) (*M B6–7*) What the Crimea is to the Russians, Bodrum (pop. 130,000) is to the Turks: a long tradition synonymous with the most beautiful weeks of the year.

It was the writers who emigrated from Istanbul that gave the city – the ancient Halicarnassus – with its castle and whitewashed houses, its legendary reputation. The bay, the illuminated castle and the picture-perfect backdrop of the harbour have always exerted a strong attraction. In 337 BC the Persian satrap, Mausolos

Photo: Bodrum with its Crusader castle

From Istanbul via Kuşadası to Bodrum: seaside resorts and the most important sites of antiquity

moved his residence to Halicarnassus. He expanded the settlement into a large city and fortified it with a 6km/3.7mi long wall; some of its remains can still be seen to this day. His tomb, the *Mausoleion*, was one of the Seven Wonders of the Ancient World. Only the foundations remain of what was once a 50m/164ft high monument (it is signposted). Bodrum bursts at its seams in the summer and the 'St

Tropez of Turkey' is especially popular with British tourists. If you want to rest, you should avoid coming here, or you should rather stay at one of the quieter bays on the peninsula. Visitors to Bodrum will enjoy slightly cooler water, good wind conditions for sailing or surfing, wonderful sunsets as they dine by the seaside and hot nights to dance the night away. A small but adequate pebble beach has

Off on a 'Blue Voyage' in the Mediterranean: a skipper on a traditional wooden sailing boat

recently been created behind the castle in the village itself. At the beginning of September the *Bodrum Festivali* takes place – an art and cultural programme with a Turkish star cast – and in October the Bodrum harbour hosts a *gulet* regatta.

SIGHTSEEING

BODRUM SUALTI ARKEOLOJI MÜZESI (UNDERWATER MUSEUM)

Turkey's only ● *Underwater Museum* is located in a beautiful medieval Crusader castle with spectacular views. The glass collection is the fourth largest in the world. The displays include ancient wreckage parts, amphorae and gold and ivory jewellery. *Tue–Sun 9am–7pm and 1pm–7pm | entrance 10 lira | www.bodrum-museum.com*

ZEKI MÜREN MUSEUM

The famous Turkish singer and actor Zeki Müren (1931–96) lived here into the 1980s. Even though he never openly declared he was gay, the singer was banned from the movies for a little while after the military coup in 1980. He was one of the celebri-

ties who made Bodrum into a refuge for bohemians 30 years ago. His home has been preserved as a museum for Turkish contemporary culture. *Tue–Sun 10am–5pm | Zeki Müren Cad. 11*

FOOD & DRINK

BODRUM FENERI

Fatih Ariman and Sami Caner have opened a fine restaurant in the marina at the end of the promenade at the small lighthouse. The pool is open in the afternoons. Accompanied by jazz music, you make your way with an aperitif to the dining room. The beautiful bay with the illuminated castle serves as a perfect backdrop. Reservations essential! *Daily 9am–2am | Neyzen Tevfik Cad. Milta Marina Fener İşletmeleri | tel. 0252 313 06 68 | Expensive*

CHINESE INN

Light, friendly and reasonably priced. Lunch buffet with large selection for about 12 lira. Peking duck and other dishes are available at lunchtime as well as in the evenings, also à la carte. *In the shopping centre Oasis above the town (dolmus buses from the city centre) | Oasis Kültür Alışveriş ve Eğlence Merkezi | Kare Avlu | Kıbrıs Şehitleri Cad. | Mon–Sat 10am–10pm | www.chineseinnrestaurant.com |* Budget–Moderate

INSIDER TIP TRANÇA

Behind the castle, on the pub mile *Cumhuriyet,* you can dine on the pebble beach at the sea. In addition to fish dishes the restaurant also serves Ottoman cuisine. Award-winning chef Emre Ulug's speciality is zander in a broth with almonds. Also vegetarian options and pizza and pasta at lunchtime. *Daily 11.30am–2am | Cumhuriyet Cad. 36 | tel. 0252 316 66 10 | www.trancarestaurant.com |* Moderate

SPORTS & ACTIVITIES

'BLUE VOYAGE' ★

The holiday trips on motorised wooden boats or *gulets* are known as 'Blue Voyages'. They can last a day or several weeks. Price: between 550 and 1350 lira per person/week. *Barbaros Yachting | Neyzen Tevfik Cad., Saray Sok. 4 | tel. 0252 316 39 19 | GSM 0533 600 15 00 | www.barbarosyachting.com (with price list)*

DIVING

The Bodrum coast, with its off-shore islands, is considered an excellent diving haunt. A good address: *Crystal Tours Diving Centre | in the Oasis shopping centre | Kıbrıs Şehitleri Cad. | tel. 0252 317 16 17 | contact person: Pertev Kandilci | www.crystaltours.com*

ENTERTAINMENT

Bodrum has the largest open air disco, *Halikarnas,* which can accommodate 5000 guests *(33 lira | Cumhuriyet Cad. 178 | www.halikarnas.com.tr)*. Next door *(no. 175)* is *Café Mavi*, Bodrum's oldest music pub. The INSIDER TIP Bodrum Jazz Days takes place from 15–31 May in *Hadigari (Dr. Alim Bey Cad. 37 | www.hadigari.com.tr)*. The *Küba Bar* at the marina *(Neyzen Tevfık Cad. 62 | www.*

MARCO POLO HIGHLIGHTS

★ 'Blue Voyage'
Cruise the Mediterranean in a *gulet,* a traditional wooden sailing boat → p. 35

★ Assos
Picturesque Aegean village with an ancient past → p. 40

★ Bozcaada and Gökçeada
Popular islands with Greek flair → p. 41

★ Troy
Where Heinrich Schliemann discovered the remains of Homer's city → p. 41

★ Hagia Sophia
The magnificent mosque in Istanbul has been a museum since 1934 → p. 42

★ Topkapı Palace
The seat of the Ottoman Empire → p. 43

★ Ephesus
The ruins of one of the most beautiful ancient cities → p. 48

★ Pamukkale
Warm springs feed the natural pools of the famous terraces → p. 49

kubabar.com) overlooks the illuminated castle and is a classy venue.

WHERE TO STAY

BAÇ PANSIYON

One of Bodrum's oldest hostels may be located in the city centre but it is still quiet. With a small beach and breathtaking view of the castle this is a good (and affordable) choice. *10 rooms | Cumhuriyet Cad. 14 | tel. 0252 3 16 16 02 | Budget*

HOTEL GULET

This nondescript, boxy building is located behind the castle, 1km from the city centre at the *Müren Museum* and has three advantages: the stunning views of the city and sea from the ⚜ front rooms, the beach right on your doorstep and reasonable prices. Terrace overlooking the sea. *24 rooms | Cumhuriyet Cad. 177 | tel. 0252 316 66 36 | www.bodrumguletotel.com | Moderate*

THE MARMARA BODRUM

This luxury hotel has the nicest swimming pool in Bodrum and it overlooks the town. Everything from a spa to tennis is available. *100 rooms | Suluhasan Cad. Yokuşbaşı Mah. | tel. 0252 3 13 81 30 | www.the marmarahotels.com | Expensive*

INFORMATION

Barış Meydanı (right in front of the castle) | tel. 0252 3 16 10 91 | www.bodrumpages. com | www.bodrum-info.org

WHERE TO GO

GÜMÜŞLÜK (128 B4) (*ⓜ B6–7*)

Small village on the tip of the Bodrum peninsula that is popular with sailors and surfers. The restaurants on the beach serve the best fish. Try the INSIDER TIP

sıcak halva for dessert! A good accommodation option is *Sisyphos* on the beach. *(21 rooms | tel. 0252 3 94 30 16 | Budget) | dolmuş from the bus station Bodrum (Otogar) | 20km/12.4mi*

BURSA

(121 E4) (*ⓜ D3*) Turkey's fourth largest city (pop. 2 million) was once on the caravan route between Europe and Asia. In addition to trade and industry, the thermal baths and winter tourism shape the face of 'green Bursa' today. Their thermal baths are by far the best in the country.
After being conquered by the Ottomans in 1326, Bursa became the first capital of the expanding empire. Bursa owes its name to the sultans as ancient Prusa was named after King Prusias I of Bythinia (200 BC) and the 'Yeşil' or 'green' is reference to its many parks and gardens. Many of the famous Ottoman buildings are clad in blue-green İznik tiles. The leafy city at the foot of the 2543m/8343ft high Uludağ deserves its 'green' title. The healing powers of Bursa's hot springs have been lauded as far back as Roman times. Almost all the thermal baths are in Çekirge neighbourhood.
The western Anatolian provincial city grew into a significant industrial city after the republic was founded. Bursa is famous for its silk processing but it is also known worldwide as the home of the invention of the kebab on a rotating spit (*döner* means 'turning'). In recent years the university has changed the face of the city.

SIGHTSEEING

KOZA HANI (COCOON BAZAAR)

The charming two-storey complex has been used as a silk trading centre for more than 500 years. In June and July farmers bring bags full of white silkworm cocoons here to be spun. Today finished silk fabrics are sold in the bazaar shops. The gardens in front of the bazaar are where the locals like to meet up for a cup of coffee. *Next to the Ulu Camii Park*

(Yeşil Camii), named after the green faience tiles which cover the two domes and parts of the interior, has a T-shaped ground plan. The *Yeşil Türbe*, Mehmed I's 25m/82ft high mausoleum, is situated on the opposite hill. The largest of nine sar-

Oriental splendour: colourful faience tiles decorate the Green Mosque

ULU CAMII (GRAND MOSQUE)

In contrast to later mosques, the 'Grand Mosque' (1400) has 20 domes of equal size, instead of one main dome. Also of interest are the prayer niche and the 16th century Ottoman stone work. The Ulu Camii in Bursa is the Turkish mosque with the greatest indoor prayer area. The Blue Mosque, or the Süleymaniye, in Istanbul only has a greater surface area with its courtyard. *Atatürk Cad.*

YEŞIL KÜLLIYE (GREEN COMPLEX)

The area in the east of the city is Turkey's most important Ottoman cemetery complex. This magnificent property from the 15th century was owned by Mehmed I and consists of a mosque, a *medrese* (religious college) and his tomb. The *Green Mosque*

cophagi belongs to the sultan. The rest are reserved for family members and senior staff but the tombs are empty as the deceased were buried in the ground. In the former religious school (Yeşil Medrese) *The Museum of Turkish and Islamic Art* displays, amongst others, weapons, clothing, ceramics and coins. *Tue–Sun 8am– midday, 1pm–5pm | free entrance*

FOOD & DRINK

LALEZAR

Lunchtime restaurant with good Turkish cuisine. The kebabs with aubergines, the stuffed paprika and even the strictly vegetarian dishes, are all highly recommended and cheap. *Heykel Meydanı, Ünlü Cad. 14 | tel. 0224 221 84 24 | Budget*

KEBAPÇI İSKENDER

Kebab fans take note INSIDER TIP *İskender Kebap* with yoghurt as a sauce was invented here, apparently named after its inventor, İskender Efendi (Mr Alexander). *Ünlü Cad. 7 | Heykel | tel. 0224 2 21 46 15 | Moderate*

THERMAL BATHS

The water which is rich in sulphur and iron is believed to help with rheumatism and gallstones. The oldest bath is the *Eski Kaplıca* (old bath) with spring water as hot as 45°C/113°F. It dates from the 14th century, has an area for women and is situated in *Çekirge | Armutlu Meydanı | Kervansaray Hotel | entrance 10, with massage approx. 45 lira | tel. 0224 2 33 93 00*

WHERE TO STAY

ÇELIK PALAS ●

The hotel complex was commissioned by Atatürk in 1935 and was modernised in 2009. The main reasons for visiting is the thermal areas: the beautifully restored marble INSIDER TIP Turkish bath with cupola and 47°C/116°F degree hot pool is an experience! Gym equipment, massages, bio-sauna, aromatherapy *(spa daily 7am–10pm, call ahead)*. A treatment in the off season is highly recommended. *156 rooms | Çekirge Cad. 79 | tel. 0224 2 33 38 00 | www.celikpalasotel.com | Moderate*

THERMAL HOTEL GÖNLÜFERAH

Tasteful, mid-range hotel situated in the thermal neighbourhood, Çekirge, with wonderful hammam and lounge where you can hear live music from ranging from Latin to Turkish. *70 rooms | 1. Murat Cad. 22 | tel. 0224 2 33 92 10 | www.gonluferah. com | Moderate*

INFORMATION

Orhangazi Parkı | tel. 0224 2 20 18 48

WHERE TO GO

CUMALIKIZIK (121 E4) *(ꕦ D3)*

This place is within walking distance from the city centre but is often overlooked. *Cumalıkızık (10km/6mi from Bursa)* is still the way the first Ottoman rulers built it in the 14th century. The village offers a journey back through time as it is as old as the Ottoman Empire itself: 700 years. Old, crooked timber-framed houses (which

A PLACE IN THE SUN

It started in 1925 when the writer, Cevat Şakir Kabaağaçlı, was banished to Bodrum from Istanbul. However, he did not consider it a punishment and instead experienced the most productive time in his life. When friends came to visit, he invited them on boat trips along the coast and this was how the Turkish intellectuals discovered the heritage of the Greeks in Anatolia – and the *Blue Voyages* began. Today *mavi yolculuk* is one of the most popular forms of holiday on the south coast. The stolid wooden ships still have their full rigging but are usually motorised. A chef takes care of the on board catering and the captain drops anchor wherever the guests prefer. Important marinas are Antalya, Marmaris, Bodrum and Fethiye.

Skiing fun on the slopes at Bursa: in the Turkish winter sports region of Uludağ

have been renovated in recent years) characterise the settlement where the inhabitants live according to old traditions. A trekking route takes you to *Mount Uludağ*. Follow the signs after 8km/5mi on the highway to Ankara or catch a minibus from the bus station Eski Garaj. There are two clean bed & breakfasts: *Hatçe'nin Yeri (5 rooms | tel. 0224 3 72 93 51 | Budget)* and *Mavi Boncuk (9 rooms | tel. 0224 3 73 09 55 | Budget)*. The village headman has additional information *(tel. 0224 3 72 40 39)*

ULUDAĞ (121 E4) (*D3*)

The ancient Greek historian Herodotus named the 2543m/8343ft high mountain the 'Olympus' western Anatolia. After the Roman Empire converted to Christianity, monks began to build monasteries here. When Orhan (1281–1362) – son of Osman Bey and second ruler of the small principality – occupied Bursa, the monks gradually left the more than two dozen monasteries. Turkish dervishes moved into some of them. Centuries later the modernisa-

tion that came about with the founding of the republic saw the first Turkish skiers arrive. In 1933 Uludağ (sublime mountain) had its first surfaced street and the first ski hotel. Once you have taken the ⚜ cable-car *(Teleferik, signposted | daily 8am–10pm | return approx. 11 lira)* to the top, the view – in clear weather – extends all the way to Istanbul. Outside the skiing season the mountain is ideal for hikes through the densely wooded forest area, which has been declared a national park. For a comfortable stay, try the hotel *Monte Baia (186 rooms | Oteller Bölgesi 2 | tel. 0224 2 85 23 83 | www.baiahotels. com | Expensive)*.

ÇANAKKALE

(120 B4) (*B3*) **Çanakkale (population 475,000) lies where the Marmara and the Aegean Seas meet.**
The Dardanelle Strait has played an important strategic role since ancient times. Two great battles took place here: the

ÇANAKKALE

Trojan wars mentioned in Homer's Iliad and the World War I battle at the Dardanelles in 1915. It was here that Lieutenant Colonel Mustafa Kemal's legendary fame began. Today Çanakkale is the starting point for destinations such as Troy, the two Turkish Aegean islands of *Gökçeada* and *Bozcaada*, *Assos* or the *Gulf of Saros,* which is very popular among fishermen for its abundance of fish. The Mediterranean's wine and olive border runs along here as well: grapes and olives are harvested from the Gallipoli peninsula up to Bodrum. There are ferries daily that connect Çanakkale with Eceabat and Kilitbahir on the European side.

FOOD & DRINK

INSIDER TIP ► **YALOVA**

Harbour restaurant steeped in tradition with terrace and sea views; serving delicious starters and seafood specialities. *Merles | Yale Cad. Gümrük Sok. 7 | tel. 0286 2 17 10 70 | www.yalovarestaurant. com | Expensive*

WHERE TO STAY

IDA KALE RESORT
A quiet and comfortable hotel situated between the city centre and Troy, with a swimming pool by the sea and its own sandy beach. *84 rooms | Güzelyalı | tel. 0286 2 32 83 32 | www.kaleresort.com | Moderate*

INFORMATION

İskele Meydanı 67 | tel. 0286 2 17 11 87

WHERE TO GO

ASSOS ★ (120 A5) *(Ø A–B4)*
The Bay of Assos (Behramkale, pop. 1600 50km/31mi from Çanakkale) has been a secret amongst Istanbul locals for a long time. It can get quite full in the summer months, but the village is still the pearl of the Gulf of Edremit. In ancient times Assos was a famous trading centre and Aristotle also taught here for three years. The Doric *Temple of Athena* high above the city dates back to the 6 century BC *(entrance approx. 4½ lira)*. A few old warehouses were converted into beautiful hotels. The Nazlıhan Hotel is right on the harbour *(29 rooms | İskele Mevkii | Ayvacık |*

tel. 0286 7 21 73 85 | www.assosedengroup. com | *Moderate*).

BOZCAADA AND GÖKÇEADA ⭐
(120 A4) (*𝄜 A3*)

The windswept island of *Bozcaada* (previously: Tenedos, 15 square miles) is known for its wine and fresh fish. Many people from Istanbul have bought and restored houses here. *Kaikias* is a hotel in a beautifully restored building *(18 rooms | Kale Arkası | tel. 0286 6 97 02 50 | www.kaikias. com | Moderate)*. Whilst Bozcaada is increasingly becoming a chic boutique island with its small, fine beaches and lively nightlife, the big island of *Gökçeada* (Imros, 1118 square miles) remains sleepy and offers its more solitary visitors a paradise, partly without electricity. The island is also ideal for biking and hiking. The *Barba Yorgo* pension, situated in an old Greek village, is a good starting point for an active holiday *(8 rooms, 6 apartments | Tepeköy | tel. 0286 8 87 35 92 | Budget)*. Car ferries to Bozcaada from Geyikli (50km/31mi from Çanakkale by bus from bus station/Garaj): travel time 30 min | to Gökçeada from Çanakkale 1.5 hours | www.bozcaada.info

TROY ⭐ (120 A4) (*𝄜 A–B3*)

Troy, made famous through Homer's epic 'Iliad', (Truva, 20km/12.4mi from Çanakkale) is situated at the mouth of the Dardanelles on the Aegean Sea. The first settlers arrived in 3000 BC. Troy was destroyed and built up again nine times until 500 AD. Today you can only view the sixth layer but if you expected exciting traces of the Trojan War – or even parts of the Priam's treasure – you will be disappointed. The excavations that Heinrich Schliemann began in 1870 were continued by the archaeologist Manfred Korfmann who died in 2005 and who was popular and honoured as 'Osman Hodscha' in the

The famous Greek hiding place – a model of the Trojan Horse

region. *Daily 9am–6pm excursions from Çanakkale with Troy Anzac Seyahat Acentası | entrance 15 lira | Saat Kulesi Yanı | tel. 0286 2 17 14 47 |*

ISTANBUL

🔲 **MAP INSIDE BACK COVER**
(121 D–E2) (*𝄜 D2*) **The city (pop. 12 million) built on two continents is the heart of Turkey and its economic and cultural capital.**

ISTANBUL

CITY **WHERE TO START?**
Sultanahmet Square (U D4)
(m d4): in the east is Topkapı Palace
and the Hagia Sophia, in the west
are the six minarets of the Blue
Mosque. Here you will find yourself
in the 'historical peninsula'. The
Golden Horn separates you from
Bosporus: left is the European part
with Pera, on the right is Üsküdar
on the Asian shore. You can get to
Sultanahmet on foot over the Galata
Bridge or by tram which travels between Aksaray and Kabataş.

Known as Constantinople the city was,
from the 4th century to 1453, the capital
of the Byzantine Empire. Thereafter the
Ottomans ruled and changed its name to
Istanbul and to this day it remains the
connection between the Orient and the
Occident. A trip to the metropolis should
be planned carefully: in 2010 Istanbul
was voted the European Capital of Culture
and as it has acquired a special position
between East and West, that has the hotels booked for months in advance. For
detailed information, see the Marco Polo
'Istanbul' guide.

SIGHTSEEING

AYASOFYA (HAGIA SOPHIA) ⭐
(U D4) *(m d4)*
The largest basilica of the Byzantine
Empire was inaugurated 537 AD. Mehmed
the Conqueror had it converted into a
mosque, today it is a museum. Visitors
should start on the ground floor and end
on the galleries, where there is a magnificent view of the interior. *Tue–Sun
9am–4.30pm, gallery 9am–10.30am,
1pm–3pm | entrance approx. 20 lira
(Sultanahmet)*

KAPALI ÇARŞI (GRAND BAZAAR) ●
(U C–D4) *(m c–d4)*
A stroll through the largest covered bazaar,
or the first 'shopping centre' in the world
(built 1461), is a must for every visitor to
Istanbul: 75 acres, 61 streets and 4400
shops. There are carpets, leather, jewellery
and souvenirs on offer. *Mon–Sat 8.30am–
7pm | www.capalicarsi.org.tr*

SULTANAHMET CAMII
(BLUE MOSQUE) ● (U D5) *(m d5)*
The most famous mosque in the city takes
its name from the amazing blue faience
tiles that decorate the walls and minarets.
The building was completed in 1616 and,
with its six minarets, it is one of the largest
mosques of Islam. You should take your
time to view it but it is a functioning
mosque so try not to walk around when
people are praying.

TOPKAPI SARAYI (TOPKAPI PALACE)
⭐ (U D–E4) (🕮 d–e4)

Seat of the Ottoman rulers for more than 400 years and the city's landmark. The palace grew gradually, behind the extensive walls, resulting in a confusing complex with gates, courtyards and outside pavilions. The precious items on display at Topkapi include jewellery and ceramics, a collection of weaponry, Ottoman miniatures, calligraphy and relics of the Prophet Mohammed. *May–Oct Wed–Mon 9am–7pm, Nov–April daily 9am–5pm, harem 9.30am–3.30pm | entrance 20, harem 15 lira | www.topkapisarayi.gov.tr*

YEREBATAN SARAYI
(SUNKEN PALACE) ● (U D4) (🕮 d4)

The Byzantine cistern that resembles a palace is supported by 336 Corinthian pillars, most of which are decorated with carvings. Two of them stand on Medusa heads. The cistern was built by Emperor Justinian in 532 in order to resolve the water crisis. Today concerts and other events take place here. *Daily 9am–6.30pm | entrance 10 lira | www.yerebatan.com*

FOOD & DRINK

INSIDER TIP ▶ **BONCUK**
(U D2) (🕮 d2)

Situated in a busy restaurant street. Delicious fish dishes. *Nevizade Sok. 19 | Beyoğlu | tel. 0212 2 43 12 19 | www.boncuk restoran.com | Moderate*

HACI BABA
(U D2) (🕮 d2)

Turkish cuisine in a pleasant environment. *İstiklal Cad. 49 | Beyoğlu | tel. 0212 2 44 18 86 | www.hacibabarest.com | Moderate*

Large bazaar: over 4000 stalls for customers to choose from

PESCATORE (0) (*0*)

Superb seafood restaurant on the Bosporus. Here you will find all kinds of tasty seafood. *Kirecburnu Kefeliköy Caddesi 29 A | Sariyer | tel. 0212 2 23 18 19 | www.yeni pescatore.com | Expensive*

WELLNESS

SÜLEYMANIYE HAMAMI ● (U C4) (*c4*)

The bath was built in 1550 by court architect Mimar Sinan, and is one of the most beautiful in the country. Once planned to be a part of the complex around the Süleymaniye Mosque, the bath with its stunning dome only serves as a tourist facility these days, where unisex bathing is allowed. The visit – including washing, exfoliation and massage – takes about 90 min (approx. 40 lira). *Daily 10am–midnight | Mimar Sinan Cad. 20 | Süleymaniye-Fatih | www.suleymaniyei.com*

WHERE TO STAY

PERA PALACE (U D2) (*d2*)

Opened in 2010, this belle époque building is *the* historical hotel in Istanbul. Originally built for Orient Express passengers, the hotel with its legendary bar is now one of the best addresses in the city. *150 Zi. | Meşrutiyet Cad. 52 | Tepebaşı (Beyoğlu) | tel. 0212 377 40 00 | Expensive*

SINBAD YOUTH HOSTEL (U D5) (*d5*)

Cheap, clean hostel with 92 beds in the old town. Breakfast and Wi-Fi included. *Küçükayasofya Mah. | Reşit Sok. 3–5 | Sultanahmet | tel. 0212 5 18 23 05 | www.sindbadhostel.com | Budget*

TAXIM HILL (U E2) (*e2*)

Comfortable city hotel in Taksim Square with bar/restaurant on the 9th floor. *50 rooms | Sıraselviler Cad. 9 | Taksim | tel. 0212 3 34 85 00 | www.taximhill.com | Moderate*

BOOKS & FILMS

▶ **Istanbul** – Nobel Prize for Literature laureate Orhan Pamuk recalls the city of his birth in a melancholy and atmospheric autobiographical essay. There are also anecdotes from the 1950s and 1960s and passages from the writings of travellers to Turkey.

▶ **Constantinople: City of the World's Desire, 1453–1924, 1995** – A very readable account of the city's cultural and social history by Philip Mansel. Full of fascinating anecdotes and interesting facts and revelations that gives some insight into the role Constantinople played as a meeting place between the West and the East.

▶ **Atatürk: An Intellectual Biography** – the biography by M. Sükrü Hanioglu is well researched and provides an analysis of the intellectual and social movements that shaped the statesman's ideas.

▶ **In July | Head On | Crossing the Bridge** – The award-winning German-Turkish director Fatih Akin shines a positive light on Istanbul and its inhabitants in his films (2000–2005).

▶ **Uzak** – the country has become a backdrop for various films, but its melancholy comes across most beautifully in films with Turkish directors, such Uzak directed by Nuri Bilge Ceylan (2002).

The jetty in Kanlıca on the Asian side of the Bosporus

WHERE TO GO

KANLICA ⚓ **(121 E2)** *(ᗄ D2)*

On the Asian side of the Bosporus, over-looking the water, this place is famous for its yoghurt and mocha. Kanlıca and neighbouring Çengelköy have both managed to maintain their village character – but on summer weekends it gets quite busy. Ferries regularly travel between Eminönü and Kanlıca (Boğaz).

PRINCES' ISLANDS (121 E3) *(ᗄ D2)*

In Turkish the islands are simply called *Adalar* (the islands). During the Byzantine era princes and royalty were exiled on the islands. Today they are popular with by locals as a place to escape to when they want a break from Istanbul. It takes about an hour to get to one of the nine islands, five of which are inhabited: *Büyükada, Heybeliada, Kınalıada, Burgazada* and *Sedef.* The islands are free of traffic. Ferries, motorboats and catamarans (faster) to the islands are available from Kabataş (on the European side) and Kadiköy and Bostancı (on the Asian side). *Tickets 2–7 lira | current timetable: www.ido.com.tr*

İZMİR

(128 B2) *(ᗄ B5)* **Turkey's third largest city (pop. approx. 4 million) is one of the most important harbour and trading centres and Nato's south-eastern Europe headquarters – a city with Mediterranean flair.**

The Gulf of İzmir is one of the most beautiful bays on the Aegean Sea. Once called 'pearl of the Aegean', İzmir is a metropolis

---

🏙 **WHERE TO START?**

Konak Square: starting point for every tour is the clock tower on Konak Square. Behind it lies the old town centre with the historic bazaar district of Kemeraltı. The Atatürk Bulvari, also called 'Kordon', stretches out along the sea to the north where there are many cafés and restaurants. Via Karsiyaka and Alsancak you reach Bayrakli, which is the city centre in the northern part. Collective taxis and city buses travel to Konak.

İZMİR

with strong Western influences and the industrial and commercial heart of the entire coastal region. The city's landmarks are the *Saat Kulesi* (clock tower) on *Konak Square* and the Atatürk Monument on *Cumhuriyet Square*. A must for every İzmir visit is a meal on the ● *Kordon Boyu* promenade followed by a leisurely stroll. The promenade is full of good cafés, pubs and restaurants. NB: many streets in İzmir have numbers instead of names.

SIGHTSEEING

ARKEOLOJİ MÜZESİ (ARCHAEOLOGICAL MUSEUM)
Remarkable collection of valuable artefacts from Greek and Roman times. Especially interesting is the collection of statues on the ground floor. *Tue–Sun 9am–midday, 1pm–5pm | entrance approx. 8 lira | Bahribaba Park (Konak) | www.kultur.gov.tr*

BAZAAR
The atmosphere at the Kemeraltı Bazaar doesn't come close to the busy atmosphere of the Istanbul Bazaar. The workshops are located behind the stands and the bazaar is famous for its INSIDER TIP handmade hookahs. It is also where you will find city's three oldest mosques, the *Hisar Camii* from the 16th century as well as the *Kemeraltı* and *Şadırvan* from the 17th century.

KADIFEKALE ☆
The 'velvet castle' on Mount Pagos offers a gorgeous view of the city and the bay. Built by Alexander the Great, the castle was later extended with additions by the Romans and Byzantines.

FOOD & DRINK

DENİZ RESTAURANT ☆
The best seafood restaurant in the city, on the Kordon – with fantastic sea views. In the summer you sit outside in the lovely garden. *Atatürk Cad. 188 B | Alsancak | tel. 0232 4 22 06 01 | www.denizrestaurant.com.tr | Expensive*

INSIDER TIP MANISA KÖFTECISI
Famous for their Turkish meatballs since 1870. Try the *kaşarlı köfte* prepared with Turkish Gouda. *Kıbrıs Şehitleri Cad. 93/A | tel. 0232 4 64 49 48 | Budget*

ENTERTAINMENT

BARYUM
A pub by the sea that offers a good restaurant (ground floor / *Moderate*) and a classic bar (top floor) on two levels with occasional live music and dancing until late in the evening. *Kordon | Atatürk Cad. 230 A | tel. 0232 4 63 49 02*

KYBELE
The popular pub attracts not only the young crowd with its live rock music weekends: golden oldies and Turkish pop are played just as often. It is loud, but also traditional. *Alsancak | 1453 Sok. 28 | tel. 0232 4 63 68 71*

WHERE TO STAY

İZMİR HILTON ☆
All the comforts of the Hiltons with stunning views over the bay. The *Windows on the Bay Bar (closed Sun)* and the eponymous restaurant *(daily)* on the roof have breathtaking views. Fitness centre with indoor swimming pool. *380 rooms, 9 apartments | Gaziosmanpaşa Blv. 7 | Alsancak | tel. 0232 4 97 60 60 | www.hilton.com.tr | Expensive*

KORDON OTEL
This hotel in the Pasaport neighbourhood, on the promenade, is one of İzmir's modern, well equipped, sound mid-range

hotels. The front rooms have a lovely sea views. *54 rooms, 6 suites | 1377 Sok. 9 | Alsancak | tel. 0232 484 81 81 | www. kordonotel.com.tr | Moderate*

INFORMATION

Gazi Osmanpaşa Blv. 1/1 D (at the Büyük Efes Hotel) | tel. 0232 484 21 48 | www. İzmir.gen.tr

ÇEŞME (128 A2) *(ⓜ A5)*

The seaside resort (pop. 65,000) at the tip of the peninsula is connected to İzmir by a highway and with its many hotels, restaurants, leisure activities and beaches it is *the* holiday destination for İzmir locals. You can stay at the modern *Pırıl Hotel* with its thermal bath. *(139 rooms | İnönü Mah. | Çevre Karayolu | tel. 0232 712 75 74 | www. pirilhotel.com | Moderate)*. The garden

Relaxed atmosphere of the Kemeraltı Bazaar in İzmir

WHERE TO GO

Excursions from İzmir are offered daily and include trips to the ancient sites of Ephesus, Pergamum or Kuşadası. To get to Selçuk (Ephesus and House of the Virgin Mary) you can take a train (90 min) from the main station İzmir *(Gar)*. There are buses to these destinations from the bus station *(Otogar)*, the buses are marked with the place names. Car rentals in Selçuk: *Scala Rent-a-Car | from 40 lira/day | Şirinyer-Buca | 384 Sokak 38 | tel. 0232 452 03 01*

restaurant *Kale Restoran* is in a beautiful setting near the castle ruins and serves Turkish cuisine *(tel. 0232 712 63 01 | Moderate)*. Information: *İskele Meydanı 8 (at the harbour) | tel. 0232 712 66 53*
There are inviting beaches in the nearby village of *Ilıca*, which is also known for its thermal springs. The *Biothermal & Thalasso Centre* at the *Altınyunus Hotel* offers rest and relaxation *(474 rooms, 57 apartments | Kalemburnu Mevkii | Boyalık | tel. 0232 723 12 50 | www.altinyunus.com.tr | Moderate)*.

One place that has become increasingly popular due to its charming old town is **INSIDER TIP** Alaçatı *(www.alacatiguide. org)*. The *Oda Hotel* next to the restaurant *Picante* in the centre is small but nice *(9*

Classical antiquity: the ruins of Ephesus

rooms | Kemalpaşa Cad. 67 | tel. 0232 716 72 14 | mobile phone 0 53 22 24 93 76 | www.odaalacati.com | Moderate). Buses to Çesme peninsula from İzmir from the station at the Fahrettin Altay Meydanı | June–Sept every 30 min | information: İskele Meydanı 8 | tel. 0232 712 66 53 | www.cesme.gov.tr

EFES (EPHESUS) ★ ●
(128 B–C3) (*m B6*)

The visit to the ruins *(high season daily 8.30am–7pm, low season 10am–4.30pm | entrance approx. 20 lira | www.epesos.at)* of the ancient Greek city of Ephesus (70km/ 43.5mi from İzmir) is one of the highlights of a trip to Turkey. In ancient times this financial and trading centre with a quarter of a million inhabitants was still situated by the sea. Shifting alluvial plains mean that it is now situated 10km/6mi inland – near the town of Selçuk. The ruins of the monumental *Artemis Temple* from 3rd century BC are one of the Seven Wonders of the Ancient World. Also impressive are the *theatre, gymnasium, baths, Agora* and the reconstructed *Library of Celsus*. Both the Apostle Paul and John the Evangelist are said to have spent several years in Ephesus. The *patrician houses* from 1 century AD can now also be viewed *(entrance 15 lira)*. Sightseeing in *Selçuk* (pop. 18,000) should include the remains of the *Basilica of St John*, one of the largest Byzantine churches, and the *Archaeological Museum (daily 8.30am– 5.30pm, the tourist centre is also located here)*, whose attractions include the statues of Artemis *(entrance 10 lira each)*.

A new five star hotel right on the Selçuk Pamucak beach is the *Richmond Ephesos (255 rooms | Pamucak Mevkii | tel. 0232 8 93 10 60 | www.richmondhotels.com.tr | Expensive)*. Information: *Atatürk Mah. | Agora Çarşısı 35 | tel. 0232 8 92 63 28*

The *House of the Virgin Mary*, where she is said to have died, is located 7km/4.3mi south-west of Selçuk. Its foundations apparently date back to the 1st century AD, and it is a place of pilgrimage for Muslims and Christians alike.

KUŞADASI (128 B–C3) (*m B6*)

Kuşadası (pop. 50,000, 80km/49.7mi from İzmir) is one of the main tourist attractions in Aegean along with Bodrum and Marmaris. Despite many concrete buildings Kuşadası has a lot to offer: sports and recreational facilities, hotels to suit all budgets, a modern marina, good restaurants and a dynamic nightlife. Not to mention the ancient sightseeing attractions of Ephesus, Milet and Pamukkale. There are usually several cruise ships in the harbour, so the bazaar traders have a lot of custom and the hoteliers are happy for with each guest they receive. *Kazım Usta (Balıkçı Limanı | tel. 0256 6 14 12 26 | Moderate)* is *the* seafood restaurant of Kuşadası and is right on the harbour. The *Koru Mar Hotel* on the seaside may be a large box of a building, but it is comfortable and ideally located *(272 rooms. | Gazi Begendi Mevkii | PK 18 | tel. 0256 6 18 15 30 | www.korumar.com.tr | Expensive)*.

MILET AND DIDIM (DIDYMA)
(128 B–C4) *(ᗰ B6)*

A good 100km/62mi away from İzmir are two other famous ancient sites. Milet was once the largest of the Ionian cities, a thriving trading centre with 80,000 inhabitants. It was once located on a peninsula, but is now 10km/6mi inland. The theatre stands out from the ruins, the rest are in the Pergamum Museum in Berlin, Germany. Didyma, 18km/11mi from Milet, is the largest ancient temple complex in Turkey. The Oracle of Apollo temple at Didyma was as famous as the one in Delphi. Many of the statues are now in the possession of the British Museum in London *(entrance 4 lira each)*.

PAMUKKALE ★ ●
(129 E3) *(ᗰ D6)*

The 'cotton castle' near the city of Denizli (235km/146mi from İzmir) is a fascinating natural spectacle: gleaming snow-white limestone terraced pools formed by the deposits from the thermal waters. The Romans that had the city of *Hierapolis* built here in the 2nd century AD, to make good use of the curative effects of the 35°C/95°F water, rich in calcium and bicarbonate. It is also worth visiting the *Theatre of Hierapolis* as well as the northern *necropolis*, which is the largest in Turkey *(entrance for both approx. 20 lira)*. You can stay at the centrally located thermal hotel *Koray (53 rooms | tel. 0258 2 72 22 22 | www.korayhotel.com | Moderate)* or a little further out of town at the *Spa Hotel Colossae Thermal* which also has thermal springs *(230 rooms | Karahayit Pamukkale | tel. 0258 2 71 41 56 | www.colossaehotel.com | Expensive)*.

PERGAMUM (128 B1) *(ᗰ B4)*

The ruins of the ancient city of Pergamum lie on a hill that rises above the Turkish city of *Bergama* (pop. 60,000, 100km/62mi from İzmir). This was the centre of the mighty Pergamene Empire (263–133 BC) where trade and arts flourished. Its library with 200,000 scrolls was famous and parchment (paper thin, limed animal skin) was invented here. Today the relief frieze of the Pergamum Altar is housed in the Pergamum Museum in Berlin. The Turkish government as well as the people of Bergama have tried in vain to this ancient showpiece, which was taken away at the end of the 19th century by Carl Humann. The dispute continues to this day.

But even without the altar there is a lot to admire, such as the *Acropolis (entrance approx. 20 lira)* and the steeply sloped ☆ *Asklepion Theatre (15 lira)* with an auditorium that can accommodate up to 15,000 people in the 80 rows of seats. The *Archaeological Museum* has statues and a large coin collection *(Tue–Sun 9am–midday, 1pm–5.30pm | entrance approx. 6 lira | Cumhuriyet Cad. 6 | tel. 0232 6 31 28 83)*.

SOUTH COAST

The centre of the 800km/500mi long Turkish Riviera is Antalya: over 10 million tourists visited the city and its surrounds in 2010. Long, sandy beaches and the majestic backdrop of the Taurus Mountains set the scene for holidaymakers.

The landscape is blessed with a vast number of sites from ancient times and coastal towns that lose none of their appeal even in the bustle of the holiday rush. The swimming season extends from March/April to beginning December. The most exquisite part of the Turkish Mediterranean coast lies between Marmaris and Antalya: the ancient Lycia (its major growth was around 1400 BC,) which you can explore on the Lycian Way hiking trail (e.g. with *Deep Nature Tours* in Istanbul, *tel. 0212 2 43 68 85 | www.deepnature.com)*. The coastline alternates between cliffs, peninsulas, beaches and lagoons while there are pine forests that often go right to the water's edge and secluded, small coves that can only be reached via rough, gravel roads. For more detailed information, see the MarcoPolo guide 'Turkey South Coast'.

ALANYA

(130 B–C5) (*ω F7*) **Alanya (population 120,000) is particulary popular with**

The magnificent 'Turkish Riviera' is a paradise for sun lovers and culture fans alike, it has ancient history and stunning natural beauty

Germans and about 18,000 have settled here, which is why the Turks call the city Küçük Almanya (Little Germany).

The Seljuk fortress with its miles of walls and 146 towers is the city's landmark. If you are looking for a break from the beach, you can escape to the idyllic countryside of the pine-covered mountains beneath the 2647m/8684ft high Ak Dağı peak.

SIGHTSEEING

ALANYA KALESI (FORTRESS) ⚲⚲

The citadel is on a peninsula that juts out to sea and there is a wonderful panoramic view from the western side *(daily 8am–7pm / entrance approx. 10 lira)*. The impressive *Red Tower* (Kızıl Kule), an octagonal, 35m/115ft high old tower from the year 1224, played a role in the town's fortifica-

ALANYA

Cleopatra Beach in Alanya with an imposing cliff backdrop

tion *(daily 9am–7pm | entrance approx. 3 lira)*. Also worth seeing is the Seljuk *shipyard (Tersane)* that dates back to 1227.

INSIDER TIP ▶ DAMLATAŞ MAĞARASI (STALACTITE CAVE)

A visit to this cave is especially worthwhile for asthma sufferers as the high levels of humidity, natural radioactivity and constant temperatures are believed to be beneficial. Some stalactites are 15m/49ft long. *Daily 10am–5pm | entrance 3 lira | on the north-west foot of the mountain*

FOOD & DRINK

RED TOWER BREWERY

Brewery, restaurant, pub and music hall in one. The ground floor serves as a pub that has its own brew on tap. On the first floor there is a restaurant serving international cuisine, on the second floor specialising in Turkish cuisine and lastly, on the fifth floor there is the ☀ *Sky Lounge Bar* with a guitar lounge *(from 7.30pm)*. The brewery is centrally located at the harbour. *İskele Cad. 80 | tel. 0242 5 13 66 64 | www.redtowerbrewery.com | Moderate*

WHERE TO STAY

INSIDER TIP ▶ IKIZ OTEL

The reasonably priced three star hotel looks like all the other concrete box buildings but this one is right on Cleopatra Beach and the rooms all have a sea views and free Wi-Fi. Discounts for advance bookings and single female travellers. *64 rooms | Atatürk Cad. Belen Sok. 3 | tel. 0242 5 13 31 55 | Cell phone 0 53 37 32 65 39 | www.ikizotel.com | Moderate*

INFORMATION

Next to the Damlataş Cave | Damlataş Cad. 1 | tel. 0242 5 13 12 40 | www.info-alanya. net | www.lykien.com

WHERE TO GO

ANAMUR (130–131 C–D6) (⬜ G8)

The southernmost tip of Turkey (pop. 80,000, 130km/80mi from Alanya) was an important harbour in ancient times: the Greeks built the old *Anemourion* here and you can visit the ruins 8km/5mi west of Anamur *(Tue–Sun 9am–7pm | entrance 3 lira).* East of Anamur is the *Mamure Kalesi* fortress right on the sea *(Tue–Sun 9am–midday, 1pm–5.30pm | entrance approx. 3 lira),* which was built by crusaders in the 13th century. In the district İskele there is a beach, camping and small guest houses. A comfortable place to stay is the *Vivanco Hotel (66 rooms | Kalebidi Meyydanı Bozyazı | tel. 0324 8 51 42 00 | www.vivanco hotel-anamur.com | Moderate).*

INSIDER TIP GEDEVET ☆
(130 C5) (*ḍ G7*)

High on the Gedevet Mountain (1010m/3314ft) lies the village by the same name (20km/12.4mi from Alanya), which offers great views of the sea. The *Kartal Yuvası Apart Otel* (eagle's nest) is a pleasant guest house and also the starting point for many hiking trails is a pleasant guest house and also the starting point for many hiking trails, *Kartal Yuvası Apart Otel (12 apartments | tel. 0242 5 13 71 83 | Budget).*

MANAVGAT ŞELALESI (MANAVGAT WATERFALLS) (130 B5) (*ḍ F7*)

The waterfalls are a popular tourist destination which you can approach on water from Manavgat (boat pier at the river bridge). Despite the hustle and bustle the place has its charm and the INSIDER TIP fresh trout served in the shady restaurants, next to the roaring water, tastes exceptional. *Bus and dolmuş from Side (10km/6mi) and Alanya (50km/31mi)*

ANTALYA

(130 A5) (*ḍ E7*) The tourist Mecca of Antalya, (pop. 1 million, nearly 2 million in the metropolitan area) lies on the coast of the Gulf of Anatalya. In the background is the steep snow-covered summit of the Taurus Mountain range whilst to the west the Lycian Mountains drop off sharply into the sea.

Even though millions of tourists land at the airport in Antalya, most visitors spread out to the large all-inclusive resorts along the coast on both sides of the city, so Antalya itself is not overcrowded and is made up mostly of locals. The traders and restaurateurs welcome the international guests and there is a pleasant, relaxed atmosphere in the city. The charming

★ **Kaleiçi**
The old town of Antalya is so beautiful that you should try to stay within the maze of its narrow streets → p. 54

★ **Aspendos**
The ancient Roman theatre is one of the best preserved theatres of its kind in Turkey → p. 56

★ **Ölüdeniz**
Turkey's most famous bay has azure blue waters and a white sandy beach → p. 57

★ **Patara**
The fine sandy beach is 18km/11mi long and very wide → p. 58

★ **Olympos**
One of the most beautiful beaches in Turkey and right behind it lies ancient Olympos → p. 59

★ **Dalyan**
Delightful village – rock tombs, a beach and a lake with floating forests of reeds → p. 61

MARCO POLO HIGHLIGHTS

ANTALYA

CITY **WHERE TO START?**
Saat Kulesi: the town centre is the square with the clock tower beneath the 'fluted minaret'. From here you head down Uzun Çarşı Sokak into the historic old town of Kaleiçi with its many hotels, pubs and cafés or into the nearby bazaar. Buses and *dolmuş* taxis for the beaches leave from the clock tower. The beautiful Atatürk Park on the sea is also not far from here.

character of the picturesque old town (Kaleiçi) around the harbour bay has been well preserved and many of the beautiful, traditional wooden Ottoman houses now serve as guest houses or boutique hotels.

SIGHTSEEING

ARKEOLOJI MÜZESI (ARCHAEOLOGICAL MUSEUM) ●
Dazzling display of Greek and Roman items as well as some important INSIDER TIP

prehistoric finds from the caves of Taurus. *Tue–Sun 9am–12.30pm, 1.30pm–5pm | entrance 15 lira | Cumhuriyet Cad., corner Konyaaltı*

KALEIÇI ★
The old town with its labyrinth of narrow alleys feels like an open air museum. A definite must is the impressive *Hadrian's Gate* (160 AD, *Cumhuriyet Cad.*) and the symbol of Antalya, the 1220 *fluted minaret (Yivli Minare | Atatürk Cad.)* beneath the 19th century clock tower. From the the clock tower square *(Saat Kulesi)* one of the main streets, Uzun Çarşı Sokak, leads through the old town to the harbour where there is a row of restaurants. The philanthropic Istanbul couple, Suna and İnan Kiraç founded the *Kaleiçi Museum*, an ethnographic museum housed in a restored historic Turkish house. The second building in the museums's garden was previously an Orthodox church and now serves as an exhibition space for the couple's private collection. Connected to the museum is the Research Institute on Mediterranean Civilisations. *Thu–Tue 9am–midday, 1pm–*

Antalya's old town nestles around the natural harbour basin

6pm | free entrance | Kaleiçi Barbaros Mah. Kocatepe Sok. 25 | www.kaleicimuzesi.com

FOOD & DRINK

HISAR ☼

Restaurant serving international cuisine, has a fantastic view and is situated right above the harbour. *Kaleiçi | Cumhuriyet Cad. | tel. 0242 2 41 52 81 | Expensive*

TEA GARDENS ☼

Tophane and *Mermerli (Cumhuriyet Cad., at the old town wall)* have a wonderful views of the harbour and offer reasonably priced snacks.

SPORTS & ACTIVITIES

'BLUE VOYAGE'

The boat trips go along the coast as far as Fethiye in the west. Along the way you visit places like Kaş and Kekova, once significant Lycian cities. Diving or snorkelling in the waters around Kekova you can see some traces of the ancient settlements. *Deniz Yat | Fener Mah. 1996 Sok. B 7/1 | tel. 0242 3 23 55 56 | www.denizyat. com.tr*

RAFTING

Companies offer wild water rafting trips (various degrees of difficulty) on the Köprüçay River, e.g. *Med Raft | Yeşilbahçe Mah. Portakal Çiçeği Bulvarı, Hüseyin Kuzu Apt. 14/3 | tel. 0242 3 12 57 70, 3 12 10 62 | www. medraft.com*

ENTERTAINMENT

CLUB 29

The massive open air disco and restaurant on the harbour is a trendy meeting place so dress accordingly; the view and atmosphere are worth it! *Entrance 30 lira | Liman | Kaleiçi*

MR WHITE'S BAR

Antalya's largest bar. Live music every evening. *İskele Cad. 31–33*

WHERE TO STAY

THE MARMARA ANTALYA

New, chic hotel by the seaside with lots of sports and fitness facilities. Disco and entertainment in the evenings. *238 rooms | Eski Lara Caddesi | Şirinyalı Mah. 136 | tel. 0242 2 49 36 00 | www.talya.com.tr | Expensive*

TÜTAV TÜRK EVI

Beautifully restored hotel in the old town, with a swimming pool on the patio. The hotel was established with the help of the 'Turkish Cultural Foundation' and is made up of a row Ottoman mansions and is furnished in the classic Turkish style. *20 rooms | Mermerli Sok. 2 | Kaleiçi | tel. 0242 2 48 65 91 | www.tutav.org.tr | Expensive*

LOW BUDGET

▶ In the *Plaj Oteli* at Cirali an overnight stay for two costs only 60 lira, there is also a large garden with hammocks. *10 rooms | Cirali Plaj Mevkii 2 | Kemer | tel. 0242 8 25 71 14 | www.plajotel. com*

▶ Be on the quay in Kaş at around 8am, purchase a ticket on the boat and be at the lake by 10am! For 10 lira you get a ride to Kekova and a lunch of grilled chicken, salad and fruit is included in the price. Various providers, e.g. *Likya | Kas Liman.*

ANTALYA

INFORMATION

Cumhuriyet Cad. Özel İdare Altı 2 | tel. 0242 2 411 47 | www.antalya.de | www. antalya.bel.tr

dates back to Roman times leads over the upper part of the ravine, while below the effervescent Köprüçay River is lined with numerous restaurants. If you come without a canoe, you can swim in the

No other ancient theatre in Turkey is as well preserved as Aspendos

WHERE TO GO

ASPENDOS ★ (130 A5) (*ØJ F7*)

Aspendos (50km/31mi east of Antalya) is considered one of the best preserved Roman theatres of the ancient world and can accommodate 30,000. In June a ballet and opera festival takes place in this unique venue *(entrance 15 lira)*. Also worth a visit are the remains of a Roman *aqueduct*, which you can see from a small hill near the theatre.

INSIDER TIP KÖPRÜLÜ KANYON MILLI PARK (KÖPRÜLÜ CANYON NATIONAL PARK) (130 A–B4) (*ØJ F6–7*)

This scenic landscape (50km/31mi from Antalya) is a wonderful change from the beach. A narrow stone bridge *(köprü)* that

clear, cool waters. About ◄◄ 10km/6mi higher up lie the remains of the ancient theatre of *Selge (entrance approx. 4 lira)* on a breathtaking plateau where the local inhabitants still use parts of the terraces for crops. *www.mugla-turizm.gov.tr*

PERGE (130 A4) (*ØJ E7*)

One of Anatolia's largest ancient Greek cities is today an impressive open air museum. The stadium, once the show arena for gladiator fights, is the best preserved in Turkey. The ruins are broadly scattered; they are classified and await their reconstruction and funders to sponsor the rebuild. You won't find any shade in Perge, so a hat or umbrella are essential. *Daily 8am–6pm | entrance 15 lira | towards Alanya and Aksu, from there 3km/1.8mi (signposted) | depart from the bus station (Garaj) Antalya*

INSIDER TIP ▶ **TERMESSOS** ☞
(130 A4) *(𝄞 E7)*

Between steep limestone cliffs, at a height of 1000m/3281ft, lies the ancient city of Termessos, named 'Eagle's Nest' by Alexander the Great. Some highlights of the ruins are a theatre, the Agora and a necropolis *(entrance 8 lira)*. *Dolmuş and tours starting from Antalya (30km/16.5mi)*

FETHIYE

(129 E5) *(𝄞 D7)* **The largest town on the Lycian coast (pop. 72,000) lies on a picturesque sea gulf. An earthquake in 1957 destroyed large parts of the old town.**

Unlike the large tourist centres of Bodrum, Marmaris and Antalya, Fethiye remained undiscovered for a long time. An English woman married to a Turk ran the first campsite at the beach of Ölüdeniz in the 1970s and attracted many backpacker tourists to the town. Once known as an isolated paradise, today Ölüdeniz is one of the most visited beaches in Turkey and the more conservative residents have become accustomed to the sight of the visitors from abroad and earn a good living from them – with large greenhouses in the hinterland. With its lively nightlife Fethiye now feels more like Bodrum. The town has a large marina and is the starting point for Jeep or bus tours to the surrounding bays such as Ekincik or to the valleys in the Taurus Mountains.

SIGHTSEEING

KAYA MEZARLARI (ROCK TOMBS)

The Lycian tombs – carved into a steep cliff face on the outskirts of town – are certainly worth a visit. They are considered to be the best preserved examples of their kind. ☞ A staircase at Kaya alley (near the bus station) leads up to the largest and most beautiful of the tombs, the *tomb of the Amyntas (entrance approx. 6 lira)*. Lycians preferred to bury their dead up high – in this way they were closest to the gods.

FOOD & DRINK

RAFET ●

The best restaurant on the harbour promenade has been going since the 1950. Fish specialities and Turkish cuisine. You can't go wrong here! *Kordon Boyu | tel. 0252 6 14 11 06 | Moderate*

WHERE TO STAY

HILLSIDE BEACH CLUB

A fantastic location on its own private bay: appealing architecture, spacious rooms, wonderfully clear water. *330 rooms | Kalemya Koyu | tel. 0252 6 14 83 60 | www.hillsidebeachclub.com.tr | Expensive*

INFORMATION

Opposite the pier | tel. 0252 6 14 15 27 | www.fethiye.net

WHERE TO GO

ÖLÜDENIZ ★ (129 E5) *(𝄞 D7)*

This azure blue lagoon and its white sandy beach, surrounded by trees, is 12km/8mi from the centre and famous the world over. The water is often still, and may be cloudy but it's clean. The lagoon sand can be very muddy, which is why small children shouldn't be allowed to swim here without supervision. Where Ölüdeniz is on the open sea the sparkling water is a beautiful blue-green colour fringed by forests. The surrounding coastal region is partly developed and the oldest (and nicest) hotel is also the only one right on the lagoon, the *Hotel Meri (94 rooms | tel. 0252 6 17 00 01 | www.hotelmeri.com | Moderate).*

From Ölüdeniz *dolmuş* boats offer trips to ● INSIDER TIP Butterfly Valley *(Kelebek Vadisi).* This bay owes its name to the large butterfly colony that populates the valley slopes. There is only one accommodation option *(tel. 0555 632 02 36, office in Fethiye: 0252 613 14 55 | www. kelebeklervadisi.org | Budget)* with reasonably priced small wooden bungalows and tents by the sea (half board). Electricity is available from a generator that comes on three times a day. The night sky here is wonderful, full of stars and shooting stars.

PATARA ⭐ (129 E6) (*ω D7–8*)

On the coastal road to Kaş the landscape changes suddenly and it looks like the desert has met the ocean. This is where Patara Beach (80km/49.7mi south-east of Fethiye) stretches out for 18km/11mi: the most beautiful beach in Turkey! Behind

the dunes lie the ruins of the ancient Lycian harbour of Patara that include a theatre, a city gate and a shipyard *(entrance 5 lira)*. There is a ban on building at the beach but you can still spend the night at the small hotel *Dardanos (14 rooms | tel. 0242 843 51 51 | www.pataradardanoshotel. com | Budget).*

SAKLIKENT (129 E5) (*ω D7*)

A spectacular canyon (accessible by foot), which cuts deep into the mountains with a clear stream flowing through it. The impressive natural display is especially exciting for the young ones! *Entrance approx. 4 lira | 40km/25.8mi south-east of Fethiye*

XANTHOS (KINIK) (129 E5) (*ω D7*)

The site near the village of Kınık (50km/ 31mi south-west of Fethiye) was once Lycia's most important city. Of interest are its unique pillars, like those on the *Harpy Monument* (around 480 BC) where the urns are on top of a free-standing pedestal. Harpies are bird sirens that carried the soul of the dead to heaven. Aside from

Robinson Crusoe for the day: canoeing in Patara bay

the tombs there is also a well preserved city wall, a theatre and the remains of the acropolis. The original of the famous tomb, the Nereid Monument, is in the British Museum in London *(entrance 4 lira)*.

KAŞ

(129 E6) *(∅ D8)* **Kaş (pop. 10,000) does not have any sandy beaches and has therefore remained a tranquil little Mediterranean town.**

The Greek houses of the old town, with their covered wooden balconies, make the village charming. Some restaurants on the harbour have wooden platforms so that guests can jump straight into the water, making them the ideal place to while away the evenings enjoying some fish with the harbour lights twinkling in the background. The town is also popular amongst more alternative Turkish tourists. Worth a visit is the *hyposorion sarcophagus* from the end of 4 BC and the remains of the Hellenic theatre in the west of the town. Kaş is also a popular diving centre due to the large number of wrecks off the coast.

FOOD & DRINK

BI LOKMA
In 'Mama's kitchen' a mother and daughter team cook up good Turkish home-style meals. The breakfast, the *börek* puff pastry and the aubergine puree side dish are all highly recommended. Lovely view over the harbour at sunset. *Hükümet Cad. 2 | tel. 0242 8 36 39 42 | Budget*

MERCAN
The speciality here is the INSIDER TIP 'sword fish, grilled in front of the guests – also with views over the harbour. *Yat Limanı | tel. 0242 8 36 12 09 | Expensive*

WHERE TO STAY

AQUARIUS
Beautiful sea views, large pool and a wooden platform, from which you can jump straight into the sparkling sea. *36 rooms | Ccedilukurbağ Yarımadası | tel. 0242 8 36 18 96 | www.aquariusotel.com | Moderate*

INFORMATION
Cumhuriyet Meyydanı 5 | tel. 0242 8 36 12 38

WHERE TO GO

KEKOVA (129 F6) *(∅ D–E8)*
Boats leave from Kaş (takes about 2.5 hrs) out to the fishing village *Kaleköy/Simena*. In the clear waters of the bay upstream there is a INSIDER TIP 'sunken city' with pillars, stairs and several walls. A museum for divers!

Until a few years ago the village of *Kaleköy* (ancient Simena) with its medieval castle, was virtually undiscovered by tourists. Nowadays excursion boats come here in summer, which is why it is better to visit in spring or autumn. You will have peace and quiet here, but not always electricity and warm water. The guest houses on the sea have beautiful decks where you can sit in the evenings, eating and chatting. Salih's ● *Kale Pansiyon* is recommended *(11 rooms| tel. 0252 8 74 21 11 | www.kale pansiyon.com | Budget)*.

OLYMPOS ★
(130 A5) *(∅ E7)*
An enchanted site (110km/63mi east of Kaş) with a beautiful beach. About an hour's walk away is *Chimaira* – known in Greek mythology as the eternal flame as flames are constantly fed by gas escaping from the mountain. In ancient times it was

believed to be the home of a fire-spitting dragon. Pebble beach. *Entrance 4 lira | towards Antalya 3km/1.8mi before Ulupınar in the direction of Çıralı | signpost to Olympos*

MARMARIS

(129 D5) *(*Ø *C7)* **When summer comes, the harbour town (pop. 30,000) transforms into a busy holiday resort, where there is too much of everything: hotels, restaurants, sports and leisure activities – and nightlife.**

Large sections of the city are unfortunately quite built up and only the marina is picturesque. The old ● marina *(Eski Liman)* and new marina have some lovely cafés and pubs, where you can eat inexpensively during the day and while away some time admiring the views of the Taurus Mountains. Despite the fact that Marmaris is so crowded, it has managed to keep its charm. It is also a good starting point for excursions to mountains, bays and peninsulas like Bozburun and Reşadiye. In the green hinterland you can still smell the unusual aroma of sweet gum trees. Marmaris is – along with Bodrum and Fethiye – a centre for *gulet* boat charters (the 'Blue Voyages').

FOOD & DRINK

BEGONYA
A wonderfully quiet place in the centre of the city. The menu is a blend of Turkish and European cuisine. *Hacı Mustafa Sok. 101 | tel. 0252 4 12 40 95 | Expensive*

MAYMI ●
Mustafa (MA), Yilmaz (Y), Meltem (M) and Isa (I) are the names of the young and eager hosts at this beach restaurant. Besides a stunning ⚡ sea view they also

have free sun loungers, excellent food and grills for those who want to barbecue. You can buy your barbecue meat at the restaurant. *Uzunyali Cad. 128 | tel. 0252 4 13 13 43 | Moderate*

SPORTS & ACTIVITIES

'BLUE VOYAGE'
Arya's beautiful wooden yacht 'Nostalgia' is legendary (60ft long, 4 cabins, per person from 600 lira/week with crew) and ideal for a one or two week cruise to the Greek islands (for timetable see website). *Arya Tours | Yat Limanı | Barbaros Cad. 45 | tel. 0252 4 13 43 58 | www.arya tours.de/en/start_e.php*

MOUNTAIN BIKING
Specialists for mountain bike tours (various degrees of difficulty) are available at *Active Tours (Kenan Evren Blv. | Paşabey Hotel | tel. 0252 4 13 97 86).*

WHERE TO STAY

ADRIENNE'S HOUSE
The small comfortable guest house is on the outskirts of the village of Turunç and even boasts a swimming pool. *5 rooms | Gülhak Mah. | 41 | Turunç (20km/12.4mi from the city centre) | tel. 0252 4 76 79 51 | Moderate*

DIVAN MARES HOTEL
The large property with spacious lawns offers everything you need for a perfect holiday, including a swimming pool and tennis courts. *252 rooms, 9 suites, 159 apartments | Pamucak Mevkii | tel. 0252 4 55 22 00 | www.mares.com.tr | Expensive*

INFORMATION

İskele Meyydanı 12 | tel. 0252 4 12 10 35 | www.marmaris-online.com

WHERE TO GO

DALYAN ⭐
(129 D5) *(ᗰ C7)*

This delightful town (pop. 3000, 80km/ 49.7mi from Marmaris) lies on the Dalyan River delta. The reed-lined river mouth and the wonderful bathing beach (İztuzu) upstream are all part of a nature reservation and this area is one of the last breed-

in the middle of the wilderness on the uninhabited side.

DATÇA AND BOZBURUN

West of Marmaris (by minibus) the INSIDER TIP Reşadiye and Bozburun pen- insulas extend out into the Aegean. The fishing village of *Datça (128 C5) (ᗰ B7)* (80km/49.7mi from Marmaris, pop. 15,000) with a beautifully restored old

Excursion boat riding through the River Dalyan reeds at Kaunos

ing grounds for *Caretta caretta* or Logger- head turtles. The charming village has numerous small hotels, the *Happy Caretta Hotel* is right on the river *(Maraş Mah. | Ada Sok. | tel. 0252 2 84 21 09 | Moderate)*. *Gerdas Café* belongs to an expat German who makes delicious waffles in her gar- den *(Karakol Sok. 4 | tel. 0252 2 84 36 64 | Moderate)*. From Dalyan you can take a minibus to the neighbouring *Lake Köyceğiz* via the village of Köyceğiz (about 50km/ 31mi). From the harbour you can make a boat trip to the ● INSIDER TIP hot springs

town lies on the Reşadiye. The route be- tween Marmaris and Bozburun is spec- tacular: an alpine panorama with deep blue bays. The route takes you past rivers, streams, waterfalls and old plane trees. At its end is *Bozburun (128–129 C–D5) (ᗰ C7)*, 50km/31mi from Marmaris. The hotel *Aphrodite* on the water can only be reached by boat *(20 rooms | tel. 0252 4 56 22 68 | Budget)*. You can also stay over- night and eat well at *Möwe (in the centre | tel. 0252 4 56 26 61 | www.moewe-tr.com | Budget)*.

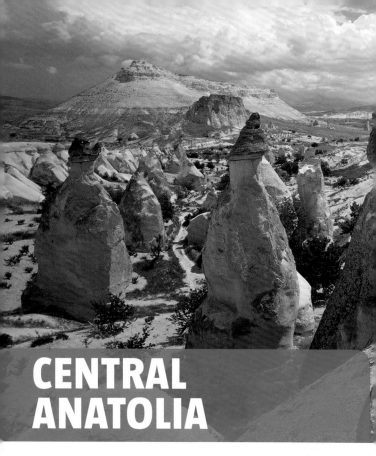

CENTRAL ANATOLIA

The barren Central Anatolian plateau stands in stark contrast to the mountain forests of the Black Sea region and the lively coastal areas in the south. Their infinite vastness and the variety of earth tones and forms seem like a copy of Asia's steppe lands, where the Turkish tribes departed to the west a thousand years ago. On their arrival they found the remains of the oldest and most significant of civilisations.

Many of central Anatolia's cities have historically served as waypoints on the Silk Road, or other trading routes towards the east, and are full of splendid caravanserais (*Han* in Turkish). The mosques and religious colleges (*medrese*) that you see along the way (for example in Konya) include some of the best examples of Islamic architecture. Anatolia's most beautiful – and most bizarre – landscape is here in Cappadocia, where soft volcanic rock forms unique geological pillars and shapes. There are rooms, tombs and hundreds of small churches hidden in the countryside, some with colourful frescoes. In the larger cities in Cappadocia and central Anatolia the infrastructure is good but in the more remote places you have to be prepared to be bit more self-sufficient. Due to the restrictive alcohol licences in central Anatolia (also east of Ankara) there are

Photo: Göreme's landscape of 'fairy chimneys'

The capital and heartland: in the steppe landscape of Central Anatolia there are traces of an ancient civilization

now fewer and fewer restaurants that serve alcohol.

ANKARA

(122–123 C–D4) (*∭ G4*) **When the founder of the Republic, Mustafa Kemal Atatürk, decided that Ankara should be the capital of the new state, it was still a small Anatolian town (ancient Ankyra, later Angora) known for its Angora wool.** Since then Ankara has grown into a metropolis with about 4 million inhabitants. Besides government ministries, trade and administration, it has all the attributes of a modern capital: expensive shops and residential district, a diverse nightlife, a strong cultural life and respected research institutes. Three quarters of the citizens of

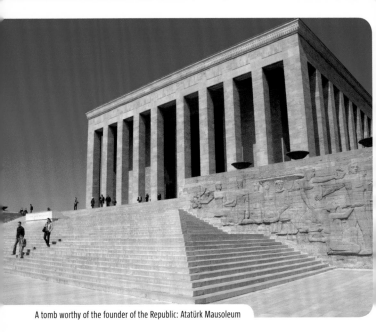

A tomb worthy of the founder of the Republic: Atatürk Mausoleum

Ankara work in the service sector. Ankara, in comparison to the vibrant Istanbul, has the reputation of being a boring city full of civil servants but the embassies and other international institutes give the city an international flair that is most noticeable in the Gaziosmanpasa and Çankaya districts.

> **CITY** **WHERE TO START?**
> **Ulus Square:** a road runs from the central square, through the old town to the citadel *(Kale)*. After your visit to the Archaeological Museum and the Atatürk Mausoleum (best by taxi) the Çankaya Hill is the next destination: here is where you will find the cafés, pubs, parks and shopping centres. You can get to Ulus by bus or taxi.

SIGHTSEEING

ANADOLU MEDENIYETLERI MÜZESI (MUSEUM OF ANATOLIAN CIVILIZATIONS) ★

This museum (also referred to as the Hittite Museum) and is a world-class antiquities museum. The complex is housed in an old bazaar and covers the time frame from the first civilisations (around 7000 BC) to the classical antiquity, with emphasis on the Hittite era (2000–1200 BC). The ancient finds are attractively arranged and presented. *May–Sept Tue–Sun 8.30am–5.30pm, Oct–April 8.30am–5pm | entrance approx. 15 lira | Gözcü Sok. 2 | Atpazarı | www.anadolumedeniyetlerimuzesi.gov.tr*

ANIT KABIR (ATATÜRK MAUSOLEUM) ●

Atatürk's landmark tomb is the symbol of Ankara. The complex includes a plaza, a park and a museum that displays personal belongings of the founder of the Republic. *Daily 9am–5pm | free entrance | Tandoğan*

KALE (CITADEL) ● ☀

The citadel towers above the city like an eagle's nest. It is not exactly clear when it was built but it is assumed to have been some time in 7th century. The walls date to Byzantine times and the Ottomans and Seljuks made further additions and renovations. The citadel's winding alleys, lined with wooden Ottoman houses, were once the heart of Angora. Most of the buildings in the area date from the 16th and 17th century and there are also many caravanserais here. At the height of the Ottoman Empire the number of the caravans on the ancient silk route increased and Ankara lay right in their path. In the southern part of the fortress is a square known for its horse market *(At Pazarı)*, which once served as the main market square. The discovery of the sea routes to Asia, and later the industrial revolution in Europe, led to Angora's demise. Today, almost 90 years after the founding of the Republic, there is still a fondness for the good old days of the Ottoman Empire and Angora. The old town has been well restored and is rich in history. *Ulus*

FOOD & DRINK

MEŞHUR İSKENDER KEBAPÇISI

The famous *İskender kebap* is served on bread with yoghurt and tomato sauce. *Paris Cad. 20 | Kavaklıdere | tel. 0312 4 18 93 00 | Budget*

VILLA

Here you will be able to indulge in Italian cuisine in a refined atmosphere – they also serve their own in-house wine. *Boğaz Sok. 13 | Kavaklıdere | tel. 0312 4 27 08 38 | Expensive*

SHOPPING

The *Karum* shopping centre next to the Sheraton Hotel in Çankaya, *Atatürk Avenue* as well as *Gaziosmanpaşa* are full of stylish shops.

WHERE TO STAY

HOTEL KEYKAN

Functional, neat, mid category hotel, centrally located near Kızılay Square; restaurant and bar. *50 rooms | Fevzi Çakmak Cad., Birinci Sok. 12 | Kızılay | tel. 0312 2 31 80 70 | www.hotelkeykan.com.tr | Moderate*

MEGA RESIDENCE HOTEL

Elegant establishment in Kavaklıdere, with spacious rooms, garden café and restaurant *Schnitzel. 30 rooms | Tahran Cad. 5 | tel. 0312 4 68 54 00 | www.mega residence.com | Expensive*

★ **Museum of Anatolian Civilizations**
The museum in Ankara is one of the great museums of the world → p. 64

★ **Cappadocia**
Cappadocia with its cave churches and bizarre landscape is a unique natural wonder → p. 66

★ **Hattusha**
The capital of the Hittite Empire is one of the most spectacular excavation sites in Turkey → p. 66

★ **Konya**
Famous as the home of Mevlevi Order and the whirling dervishes → p. 68

MARCO POLO HIGHLIGHTS

CAPPADOCIA

INFORMATION

Ankara Tourist Information Office | Gazi Mustafa Kemal Bul. 121 | Maltepe Akaray Train Station | tel. 03 12 2 29 26 31 |

WHERE TO GO

HATTUSHA ⭐ (123 F4) (*∅ J4*)

The ruins of Hattusha were discovered about a hundred years ago. The Hittite empire (about 1650–1200 BC) was one of the most important great empires of its time, and had its centre of power here, near the village of Boğazkale. You can marvel at the temple foundations, underground fortress passages as well as the Lion and King's gates, embedded in its massive ramparts. Clay tablets with cuneiform script were found in chambers that served as archives. They are displayed in the local museum. About two hours away from Ankara by car *(Tue–Sun 8am–midday, 1.30pm–5pm | entrance approx. 5 lira)*.

2km/1.2mi north-east of Boğazkale lies the rock sanctuary *Yazılıkaya* (literally 'inscribed rock') from the 13th century BC. **INSIDER TIP** Hundreds of deities are carved into the rock walls.

The bus line *Çorum Lider* connects Ankara and Hattusha *(tel. 0312 2 24 13 14)*. A recommended hotel is *Mavi Ocak* in Sungurlu. *40 rooms | Samsun Yolu 5km/3mi | tel. 0364 3 13 00 33 | www.maviocak.com.tr | Budget*

SOĞUKSU MILLI PARKI (SOĞUKSU NATIONAL PARK) (122 C3) (*∅ G3*)

The 4 square mile national park near Kızılca (about 80km/49.7mi from Ankara away, on the route to Istanbul) is a popular destination for urbanites and scout groups on weekends. The area, with its mixed forest, is more reminiscent of the forests found in the low mountain ranges in Europe (max height 1800m/5905ft). The park is ideal for hikes and is home to many wild animals such as foxes, wolves, wild boar and birds of prey. *Buses from Ankara Bus Station (Ulus) | entrance 6 lira*

CAPPADOCIA

(131 E–F 2–3) (*∅ J–K 5–6*) ⭐ In the triangle between Nevşehir, Kayseri and Niğde are massive volcanic cones of that look like they have been set up for a giant game of ten-pin bowling.

Cappadocia is Anatolia's most awe-inspiring landscape. Over a span of 60 million years rain, wind and rivers have created a surreal lunarscape out of the soft tuff stone. The ash-grey rock facades conceal homes, 360 small churches and villages that were used by the early Christians as hiding places. You can visit some of these caves and simple chapels carved into the stone. Cappadocia has in recent years developed into a chic destination and you can stay overnight in luxury in one of the boutique *cave hotels.* The surreal landscape, the uniqueness of the accommodation, horseback treks and balloon rides over the valley all make a Cappadocia holiday an adventure. Information: *Park İçi (in the park) | Ürgüp | tel. 0384 3 41 40 59 | www.cappadociaonline.com*

WHERE TO GO IN CAPPADOCIA

INSIDER TIP AVANOS (131 F2) (*∅ J5*)

The place is famous for its terracotta pots and vases. Those who want to try their hand can make their own clay pots in the potteries across from Bazaar 54 on the street that goes towards Göreme.

GÖREME (131 F2) (*∅ J5*)

In the Göreme valley there are numerous churches hewn out of rock, accessible via winding tunnels and narrow passages. The interiors are decorated with colourful fresco cycles detailing religious scenes and the life of Jesus. The oldest of the cave churches dates back to the 5th century *Göreme Açık Hava Müzesi (Open Air Museum Göreme) | daily 8.30am–5.30pm | entrance approx. 15 lira, Karanlık Kilise (cave church 8 lira)*.

One of the area's nicest guest house – with rooms carved into the rock – is the *Melek Cave Hotel (20 rooms | tel. 0384 2 71 24 63 | www.melekcavehotel.com | Budget)* while the *Ataman (20 rooms | Uzundere Cad. | tel. 0384 2 71 23 10 | www.ataman hotel.com | Expensive)* offers the best quality. At the INSIDER TIP Rainbow Ranch *(tel. 0384 2 71 24 13 | www.rainbowhorse center.com)* you can have a horse saddled up for you and head off for a ride (2hrs with guides about 80 lira). A special experience in Cappadocia is a hot air balloon ride at sunrise *(incl. champagne breakfast 200–250 lira | enquiries at Melek Cave Hotel)*.

IHLARA VADISI (PERISTREMA VALLEY) 〰 (131 E3) (*ⓜ J6*)

Don't leave Cappadocia without spending at least half a day in this canyon gorge south-east of Aksaray. The INSIDER TIP Peristrema (the twisted valley) canyon is 100m/328ft deep and 10km/6mi long, with a tree lined river cutting through it – it is massive with a scale similar to the Grand Canyon in America. The entrances to numerous churches are visible on the canyons slopes. There are three entrance points to the valley, one is at the start of the village of *Ihlara*, one in the centre of the valley (signposted and with steps going down) and one in the north near Belisırma. *Access 7am–8pm | entrance about 10 lira | www.goereme.org*

KAYMAKLI AND DERINKUYU (131 F2) (*ⓜ J5*)

Up to eight floors of underground settlements were uncovered near Kaymaklı and Derinkuyu. The sites (parts of which were

In a hot air balloon you get a bird's eye view of Cappadocia's remarkable volcanic cones

built by the Hittites) include an ingenious escape system as well as toilets, arsenals, water cisterns and churches. The underground complex meant that the inhabitants from the villages above ground could survive for a considerable time underground when under threat. *Daily 8.30am–5.30pm | entrance 10 lira each*

MUSTAFAPAŞA (131 F2) (*∅ J5*)

6km/3.7mi south of Ürgüp, on the road to Soğanlı is the small village of Mustafapaşa (once Greek Sinasos). A picturesque village (pop. 2500) was once a summer resort of wealthy Greeks and offers some lovely churches and traditional stone houses. A caravanseria that dates back to the 14th century – a reminder that Cappadocia was located on the silk route – sells hard to come by INSIDER TIP ▶ Cappadocian wine. A tip is the *Kappadokya wine cellar in the Davuthi district | tel. 0384 3 53 50 03*. The club *Natura Cappadocia* offers accommodation in an old town house *(6 rooms | Sümer Sok. | tel. 0384 3 53 50 30 | cell 0535 3 47 11 57 (Aysel Koch) | www.club natura.com | Moderate)*.

SULTANSAZLIĞI MILLI PARKI (SULTANSAZLIĞI NATURE PARK) (132 A2–3) (*∅ J–K 5–6*)

The nature park covers 66 square miles of marshland and has three lakes: Yay, Çöl and Söbe. The middle lake, Söbe, stretches 60km/37mi east of Ürgüp. The park is a bird paradise and home to almost 300 species: pelicans, cormorants, coots and herons breed in the reed beds. *Minibus from Ürgüp bus station*

UCHISAR ☆ (131 F2) (*∅ J5*)

This picturesque place is on the outskirts of Nevşehir and is dominated by an impressive rock outcrop crowned by a medieval citadel. A Frenchman has restored ten stone houses that are available as

self-catering houses or studios, *Les Maisons de Cappadoce (Semiramis A. Ş. | Belediye Meydanı 24 | tel. 0384 2 19 28 13 | www.cappadoce.com | Expensive)*. You can eat well at *Bindallı Restaurant* next to *Kaya Hotel | Ürgüp Cad. | tel. 0384 2 19 26 90 | Moderate*

ÜRGÜP (131 F2) (*∅ J5*)

The town (pop. 10,000) is the ideal starting point for your excursions in Cappadocia. It has good transport links and a variety of accommodation options. On Ürgüp's highest hill, *Temenni Tepesi* (the hill of wishes), lies the tomb of the Seljuk king *Kılıç Aslan*, whom was also esteemed by the local Christian community. When the Seljuks conquered this part of the Byzantine Empire 900 years ago, the Christians were allowed to continue living undisturbed in their caves. The *Alfina (32 rooms | İstiklal Cad. | Ürgüp Girisi 25 | tel. 0384 3 41 48 22 | www.hotelalfina.com | Moderate)* on the outskirts of town, offers unique accommodation in original cave dwellings. On a hill outside Ürgüp is the *Hanedan* restaurant where you can enjoy delicious food served on a beautiful terrace *Nevşehir Yolu | tel. 0384 3 41 42 66 | Moderate*

KONYA

(130 C3) (*∅ G6*) ★ **Konya (pop. metropolitan area 2 million) is, in many ways, a remarkable city well worth a visit.**
It is the centre of Anatolian Islam and the religion has shaped this city. It is where the world famous Mevlevi Order was founded – more popularly known as the whirling dervishes – a mystic order, which preaches tolerance and peace. One of the big attractions of the city is the annual dervish festival on 12 December, the anniversary of the death of the mystic

The annual Dervish Festival takes place in the Mevlevi Order mosque

Mevlana Celaleddin Rumi. The dervishes whirling in their trance dance makes for a mesmerizing spectacle.

Konya is a green oasis in the middle of a barren plain, and it is characterised by lush green areas fed by numerous springs and streams. Its prime location meant that the Seljuks made Konya (Roman: Iconium) the capital of their empire. There are a number of well preserved buildings that date from that time.

In recent years religion, in public life in Turkey, has become more palpable. This is a reflection of the government's new Islamic orientation. This is most evident in central and eastern Anatolia: in Konya you will be hard pressed to find a restaurant that serves liquor (besides your hotel). But the area is booming as the so-called 'Anatolian tigers' – a new breed of entrepreneurs with Islamic values from Konya, Kayseri and the surroundings – have invested in their region. Chic shopping centres, a clean and prosperous environment and a functioning infrastructure all make this a modern metropolis. In spring millions of tulips bloom on the Konya plain. They cannot compete with the highly subsidised Dutch growers and are therefore not being exported to Europe; instead they make a beautiful display in the parks and green areas of Istanbul and Ankara.

> **CITY** **WHERE TO START?**
> **Mevlana Complex:** the heart of Konya is the mausoleum of the mystic Rumi (known as Mevlana in Turkish) and the neighbouring Mevlana Museum of the Sufi Order. To the east is Alaeddin Hill with the impressive Ince Minare Mosque and south of the hill the Archaeological Museum, Melvana Street leads up the hill. You can explore all of this on foot or, if you aren't staying in the city centre, you can take a bus or taxi.

ALAEDDIN TEPESI (ALAEDDIN HILL)

The largest and oldest Seljuk mosque in Konya, the *Alaeddin Camii*, is in the middle of a park with shady tea gardens. It took seventy years to build and was inaugurated in 1221 – at the height of the Seljuk power in Asia Minor – by Sultan Alaeddin Keykubat I. The wooden ceiling is supported by 42 ancient pillars, the *mihrab* (prayer niche) is decorated with beautiful ceramic tiles and the *minbar* (pulpit) is a masterpiece of carved ebony. Across from the mosque, on the opposite side of the street, is the *Büyük Karatay Medresesi* (Great Karatay Medrese), now a *tile museum (Tue–Sun 8.30am–5pm | entrance 3 lira | Alaeddin Meydani)*. The building was built 1252 is still the most impressive of the medresses from the Seljuk era.

ETNOGRAFYA MÜZESI (ETHNOGRAPHY MUSEUM)

The exhibitions include clothing, costumes, tools and weapons from the region. *Tue–Sun 8.30am–12.30pm and 1.30pm–5.30 pm | free entrance | Larende Cad.*

MEVLANA MÜZESI (MEVLANA MUSEUM)

The monastery *(tekke)* of the dervish Mevlevi Order is the second most-visited museum in Turkey after Topkapi. The founder of the Order Celaleddin Rumi (1207–73) was born in Afghanistan and lived in Konya. He found many followers in the 13th century through his mystical beliefs and his sermons about peace and universal love. Rumi's tomb *Yeşil Türbe* (known as the 'green tomb' because of the green tiles that decorate its conical roof) is in the centre of the complex. Some highlights include 30,000 of the Order's manuscripts and the collection of carpets and kilims from the 13th–18th century. *Tue–Sun 10am–6pm | entrance 6 lira | Mevlana Cad.*

LOW BUDGET

▶ Before your visit to the Hittites you should try the *Hattushas Restaurant* in Boğazkale Çorum: a two course lunch cost approx. 12 lira. *Daily 10am–10pm | Çarşı Mahallesi | Cumhuriyet Meydanı 22*

▶ The restaurants around Kızılay Square in Ankara serve good home-style cooking. *Karadeniz Yavuz Lokantası* has a buffet on Sat/Sun for 15 lira. *Daily 9am–9pm | Silahtarağa Cad. 220 | tel. 312 2 11 24 20*

▶ Cheap and tasty *etli ekmek* (pizza bread topped with mince meat) can be enjoyed at Konya's *Şifa Restaurant. Daily 11am–10pm | Mevlana Cad. 29 | tel. 0332 3 52 05 19*

HACI ŞÜKRÜ

Kebab house serving specialities like *etli ekmek* (Turkish pizza) and the local *fırın kebap* (oven kebab). *Devri Cedid Mah. | Cem Sultan Cad. Fuar Sitesi 327/A | tel. 0332 3 52 76 23 | Budget–Moderate*

Konya's bazaar district, which extends from Cumhuriyet to Atatürk Caddesi, has a INSIDER TIP large selection of traditional handicrafts.

WHERE TO STAY

DEDEMAN

Five star hotel with all creature comforts, including outdoor and heated swimming pools, hammam and fitness centre. *207 rooms | Özalan Mah. | Selcuklu | tel. 0332 221 66 00 | www.dedeman.com | Expensive*

ÖZKAYMAK

An attractive four star hotel situated in a quiet location, heated pool and sauna. *108 rooms | Nalçacı Cad. | tel. 0332 237 87 20 | www.ozkaymakotels.com | Moderate*

INFORMATION

Mevlana Cad. 21 | tel. 0332 321 10 74 | www.kultur.gov.tr

WHERE TO GO

ÇATALHÖYÜK ●
(131 D3) (*m G6*)

About 40km/25.8mi south-east of Konya is one of the oldest settlements in human history. The site was excavated in the 1960s by the British archaeologist James Mellaart. In about 9000 BC more than 2500 people lived in area that covered about 50 football fields. There was a ready source of water and a correspondingly abundant supply of food (animals, wheat and fruits). The settlement covers two hills; the eastern hill is the older of the two. This is where most of the excavations have taken place; the western hill only has a single excavation section, which shows that that part was settled later. The homes were rectangular, mud-brick houses set cheek by jowl and the interiors had differing ceiling heights and floor levels which ensured insulation and ventilation. The entrance area was a hatch in the ceil-ing, with a ladder down into the dwelling, and the entrance also served as a vent for the stove.

Çatalhöyük: remains of an 11,000 year old settlement

Mellaart's excavations also revealed vivid paintings and murals on the interior walls of some homes and these depictions are one of the most spectacular records of life in Çatalhöyük. Most of the finds can be seen at the Museum of Anatolian Civilizations in Ankara, but the small local museum is also worth a visit. There is a road out to Çatalhöyük and buses from the central bus station in the *Halil Ürün Caddesi*

KIZILDAĞ MILLI PARKI (KIZILDAĞ NATIONAL PARK) (130 B3) (*m F6*)

The national park covers 2 square miles and is about 130km/81mi west of Konya. There is a lake, *Beyşehir,* and plenty of sites for camping and picnicking from May to September. *Car or bus from Konya*

SOUTH-EAST ANATOLIA

The enchanting beauty of the eastern border region of Turkey is still largely undiscovered. Majestic mountains, such as Mount Ararat (Noah's mountain) alternate between steppe-like plains and green river valleys – the Euphrates and the Tigris are the region's lifelines.

The Kurds are still the majority in the south-east. Historically the unique landscape, which stretches along the borders of Syria, Iran and Iraq, has been home to many people and cultures: Seljuk Turks, Arabs, Armenians, Assyrians and Greeks and their legacy lingers in the abandoned fortresses, monasteries and churches. Despite Ankara's best efforts to solve the Kurdish question peacefully, the fighting between the illegal Kurdish Workers' Party (PKK) and the army continues. An agreement has not yet been reached between the Kurdish leaders and the central government. Due to the the rising influence of Kurdish nationalism the region has parted ways with Ankara and the situation remains tense. Therefore tourists should exercise extreme caution and before your trip, take into consideration the safety warnings given by your Foreign Office. The ambitious South-East Anatolian Project (GAP) was meant to turn the lagging region into a verdant and lush landscape. The Turkish government invested 32 bil-

Photo: Church of the Holy Cross Ahtamar at Lake Van

The oldest cities in the country are in
the sparsely populated east – surrounded
by towering mountains

lion dollars in the project. With the help
of 22 dams on the Euphrates and the
Tigris, 6564 square miles of land is now
being watered – an area larger than the
Benelux countries. But as the decades-
long struggle brought livestock farming
almost to a standstill – and the agricultural land is concentrated in the hands of
Kurdish landowners – economic development is moving forward at a snail's pace.

The south-east remains an underdevel-
oped area with high birth and death rates,
where the modern is only slowly draw-
ing in.

In consideration of the conservative
moral code of the local population you
should always cover your arms and legs.
It is also advisible to travel on the main
roads and to stay overnight only in the
larger towns.

DIYARBAKIR

(134 A3) *(∅ O6)* **In the middle of the steppe-landscape above the Tigris lies south-east Anatolia's metropolis, a historic capital with 1.5 million inhabitants.** Most of them are Kurdish civil war refugees who fled the conflict in the last few

A richly decorated house in Mardin

years. The immigrants suffer from high rates of unemployment and populate the streets and cafés. Nevertheless, the move into the modern world is noticeable. The Dicle University and EU funds have been contributing factors to the changes. In summer you must not leave Diyarbakır without first tasting the most delicious watermelons in the world!

SIGHTSEEING

SURLAR (CITY WALL)

The basalt wall, which surrounds the city, is a very conspicuous landmark. About 5km/3mi of the city wall still stands today (the oldest in Anatolia) and visitors can walk around on it. The thick wall (12m/39ft high and 5m/15ft wide) was once reinforced with 78 towers and has its origins in 394 under Roman rule. The Arabs, Seljuks, Persians and eventually the Ottomans added to the structure. The double-towered *Harput Gate*, one of four main entrances to the city, is worth a visit. The gate hall in the interior is decorated with animal reliefs.

ULU CAMII (GREAT MOSQUE)

The Great Mosque, one of the city's landmarks and the earliest Seljuk Sultan mosque in Anatolia, was built in 1091/92 by Sultan Malik Schah, shortly after Diyarbakırin was conquered. *Gazi Cad.*

FOOD & DRINK

TAVACI SUAT USTA

Diyarbakır offers a rich cuisine with lots of lamb and pita bread fresh from the oven. The stuffed lamb ribs or lamb stew with rice are delicious! *Daily midday–11pm | Inönü Cad. 27 | Merkez | tel. 0412 2 23 12 61 | Moderate*

WHERE TO STAY

KERVANSARAY ●

Restored, 500 year old inn for caravans with a good restaurant. Also live music in the evenings. You can also eat in the INSIDER TIP cosy bar on the first floor, where it is a bit quieter. *45 rooms | Gazi Cad./Mardin Kapısı | tel. 0412 2 28 96 06 | www.diyarbakirhotels.net | Moderate*

INFORMATION

Kültür Sarayı Kat 5 | tel. 0412 2 21 21 73 | www.kultur.gov.tr

WHERE TO GO

MARDIN
(134 A–B4) (*M P6*)

Mardin (pop. 700,000) is the Arabian pearl of Turkey. About 40km/25.8mi from the Syrian border (about 100km/62mi from Diyarbakır) it lies on a ⚘ hill, with wide views over the Syrian lowland. The unique terraced site of the old town distinguishes itself with its double-storied, ornate traditional stone houses made from pale limestone. Unfortunately the centre now has quite a few new concrete buildings. A fortress dominates the city, and up the hill are some old mosques, the largest of which is the spectacular *Ulu Camii*. Mardin is a feast for the senses, especially at sunset when the limestone INSIDER TIP houses glow in the dusk. The most famous son of the city is the distinguished contemporary author Murathan

Mungan. Accommodation in historic villas is available at Erdoba Konakları. *31 rooms | Cad. 135 | tel. 0482 2 12 76 77 | www.erdoba.com.tr | Moderate*

TUR ABDIN ★
(134 B4) (*M P6*)

The region around Mardin, and further east around Midyat, is the home of the Syriac Orthodox minority, now fighting for its existence. In some villages on the border with Syria church towers still overlook the tiny houses. Only 2300 West Syriac Christians live in Tur Abdin (mountain of the servants of God). Most of them have fled for political and economic reasons. The *Deyrüzafaran* from 493 AD (from Mardin by taxi, 5km/3mi) is one of two Syriac Orthodox monasteries. Only a few monks live here. The larger and better known monastery is *Mor Gabriel,* 23km/14mi behind Midyat on the way to Cizre.

ŞANLIURFA

(133 E4) (*M N7*) **The ancient Edessa, now 50km/31mi from the Syrian border, is 3500 years old, making it one of the oldest settlements in the world.**

Urfa (the prefix *şanlı*, 'full of glory', was only added in the 1980s) survived for a long time from border trade and smuggling between Turkey, Syria and Iraq. The political circumstances, especially the Gulf wars, put an end to this but the dam project is attracting people back to the region – the population had increased to 1.6 million in 2010. At the core of the gigantic watering project is the Atatürk Dam 60km/37mi to the north. Nowadays the dam is also used for sailing and swimming making the region known for these more modern activities. Despite this the area is still traditional and you will feel as though you are in the Orient when you visit the old town with its lively ● INSIDER TIP bazaar. This also has a lot to do with the significant Arabic minority. Traditional artisans and craftsmen, such as coppersmiths, can still be found here.

SIGHTSEEING

ABRAHAM'S CAVE ●

The Muslims believe that Abraham (Turkish: İbrahim) was born in Urfa, in Abraham's grotto in the southern part of the city. This is why there are half a dozen mosques here. The most beautiful mosque is the *Halil ur-Rahman,* which was originally built in the 13th century on a Byzantine church and today shows clear Arabic influences.

FOOD & DRINK

CİĞER

The host was once a middleweight wrestling champion; now he serves the house speciality lamb liver *(ciğer)* on skewers. The dessert is an experience: *kadayif* a INSIDER TIP warm puff pastry. | *Daily 8.30am–10pm | Cumhuriyet Cad. 14 A | tel. 0414 3 15 06 52 | Budget*

WHERE TO STAY

INSIDER TIP CEVAHIR KONUKEVI ●

The most beautiful old town house belongs to the governor *(vali).* It has a quiet courtyard – where you can enjoy the soothing effects of a hookah – and a roof terrace. In the restaurant you can get the best Urfa kebab in town. *Büyükyol Cad. (opposite the Selahaddin Eyyubi Mosque) | tel. 0414 2 15 93 77 | www.cevahirkonukevi. com | Budget*

INFORMATION

Asfaltyol 4/D | tel. 0414 2 15 24 67 | Info about the GAP Project: www.gap.gov.tr

LOW BUDGET

▶ The manager of the *Kervansaray Hotel* in Diyarbakır owns a small private zoo, on the way to the Dicle University, where you can picnic in the open air with your own drinks and snacks. *Daily 10am–5pm | Özel Hayvanat Bahcesi | Dicle Yolu*

▶ In Diyarbakır you can enjoy *kadayif,* a dessert with goat's cheese, which is especially delicious here because the goats on the mountains eat a lot of thyme. Affordable and good: *Kadayifci Haci Levent (Izzet Paşa Cad. 13)*

▶ The silversmiths of Şanlıurfa are legendary craftsmen. A bangle takes five days to make and is amazingly cheap: *Emre Gümüş (Divanyolu Cad. 29/A | tel. 0414 2 16 62 79)*

HARRAN (133 E5) (*ω N7*)

In the village of Harran (50km/31mi from Şanlıurfa) INSIDER TIP beehive-shaped adobe houses have stood for centuries. The village also has the remains of of 12th century castle. The earliest settlement in Harran dates back to the 3rd millennium BC. According to the Bible, Abraham lived here for a few years before he moved on into the promised land of Canaan. The only local hotel is the *Bazda (8 rooms | Merkez | tel. 0414 4 41 35 90 | Budget)*. The tourist office is in the town hall: *Belediye | tel. 0414 4 41 20 75*

NEMRUT DAĞI (MOUNT NEMRUT) ★
(133 E3) (*ω N6*)

Two hours drive north of Şanlıurfa you can see the magnificent, giant statues of Mount Nemrut. The colossal heads mark a place of worship that was once built by King Antiochus I, ruler of Commagene (a small state 69–34 BC). The assembly has been damaged and partly destroyed by erosion, earthquakes, man and the passage of time. The heads are on the western and eastern terraces and can be marvelled at in contrasting light e.g. at sunset. If it is to be sunrise, you need to get going by about three in the morning during the summer time. At *Kahta* you can get further details: *Turizm Danışma (M. Kemal Cad. 52 | tel. 0416 7 25 50 07)*. There is also a recommended hotel: *Nemrut Tur Oteli (55 rooms | M. Kemal Cad. 11 | tel. 0416 7 25 68 81 | Budget)*.

VAN

(135 E2) (*ω R5*) **The provincial capital (pop. 500,000) lies on the eastern shore of Lake Van.**

The largest lake in Turkey (120km/74.5mi long, 80km/49.7mi wide and 457m/ 1500ft deep) has a high salt content and

Huge statues of various gods on the summit of Nemrut Dağı

is suitable for swimming only under certain conditions. Framed by the peaks of volcanic mountains, it is still a worthwhile destination. The Urartian settlement was flattened by an earthquake in the 8th century BC and in WWI the old town was totally destroyed – and there is now very little left of 3000 years of settlement. The Urartians (from the Hebrew word 'Ararat') made Van the capital of their empire in 900 BC. After that the Persians, Romans and Armenians left their mark.

Van experienced a heavy earthquake catastrophe at the end of October 2011. The ongoing aftershocks made the inhabitants panic and many left the city temporarily. The wounds are slowly healing, new and earthquake-safe settlements are developing outside the old city centre.

SIGHTSEEING

VAN KALESI (CITADEL)

On the rocky outcrop in the west of the city there are fortress ruins that date back from various epochs, from the Urartians to the Ottomans. Particularly impressive are the inscriptions carved into rock, which show that the fortress of the Urartian settlement of Tuschba was situated here (9 BC). *Entrance 3 lira*

FOOD & DRINK

AHTAMAR ADASI RESTAURANT

This affordable restaurant is opposite the restored Ahtamar Church (Turkish: Akdamar) in Van, right at the Lake Van pier. *Daily | tel. 0432 6 22 25 25 | Moderate*

WHERE TO STAY

BÜYÜK URARTU HOTEL

Best hotel in the area, with an indoor swimming pool. *75 rooms | Cumhuriyet Cad. 32 | tel. 0432 2 12 06 60 | www.buyuk urartuotel.com | Moderate*

INFORMATION

Cumhuriyet Cad. 19 | tel. 0432 2 16 20 18 | www.kultur.gov.tr

WHERE TO GO

AHTAMAR KILISESI (CHURCH OF THE HOLY CROSS) ★
(135 D2) (*∅ R5*)

The landmark of Lake Van is the 1000 year old Armenian Church of the Holy Cross (oldest parts built 915–921), which looms over the Ahtamar Island in the lake. This was the seat of the Catholicos, the spiritual head of the Armenians, until 1464. The church, which is also famous for its unique, ornamental relief carvings of Old Testament scenes on the exterior walls, was restored by the Turkish government and reopened as a museum in March 2007 as a sign of reconciliation with the Armenians. *Wed–Mon 9am–5pm (Oct–May until 3pm) | minibus to the port (40km/ 25.8mi from Van past Gevaş) where small boats take you to the island*

INSIDER TIP ANI
(127 E3) (*∅ R3*)

The former Armenian capital, which was founded in the 4th century, is about 400km/248.5mi from Van making it a half a day's journey, but it is worth the effort. You can also do a detour to Doğubeyazıt, a ghost town abandoned 600 years ago. If you drive in a northerly direction to the city of Kars and follow the signs to Ocaklı, you reach the Turkish-Armenian border, and the ruins of Ani.

In the centre of the dilapidated walls and church ruins are the relatively well preserved remains of the cathedral (989–1001). Find out beforehand if the ruins are accessible *(entrance 4 lira)*. You need permission to come here, which you can obtain from the *Tourist Information Board (Orta Kapı Mah. | GAMP | Faikbey Cad. 135 | tel. 0474 2 23 35 68)* or local agents *(e.g. Seyit Turizm | Orta Kap Mah. | GAMP | Yusufbey Sok. 272/A | tel. 0474 2 12 60 46 | seyitturizm@hotmail.com)*.

However, this takes a day so it is advisable to stay overnight in *Kars*, one option is the *Motel Arkar Anihan (64 Zi. | Çevreyolu SSK Kavşağı | tel. 0474 2 12 78 00 | www. karsanihan.com | Moderate)*. Buses leave from the bus station (Garaj) in Van to Kars (364km/226mi)

DOĞUBEYAZIT
(127 F5) (*ΩΩ R4*)

This small town, three hours drive by car from Van, is home to two of the most spectacular sights of the south east: first

ever reach it. To climb Mount Ararat, you need permission from Ankara.

⊿⊾ 6km/3.7mi away is the second attraction: ★ ● *İshak Paşa Sarayı, (Ishak Pasha Palace | entrance 3 lira)* a fairytale palace that is now partly ruined. With views over the plain it towers 270m/886ft high and has an amazing 366 (!) rooms including a hammam, harem and gardens, and was built by a local prince at the end of the 18th century. In the 99 years it took to build almost all of the architectural styles of the region were referred to, from the

Last of the historic Turkish palaces: İshak Paşa's pleasure palace

and foremost is *Mount Ararat* (Turkish: Ağrı Dağı), whose 5137m/16,945ft high snow-covered peak at can be seen for miles in good weather – this mountain seems to be so high that no flood could

Armenian Georgian to the Seljuk to the Baroque Ottoman. Just outside the city is the *Simer Hotel (125 rooms | Doğu Beyazıt/ Ağrı | İran Transit Yolu | tel. 0472 3 12 48 42 | www.simerhotel.com | Moderate)*.

BLACK SEA COAST

Humid breezes blow in from the sea and there is often fog on the mountains – this is a climate where hazelnuts, tobacco and tea thrive.

A unique landscape stretches from the dark blue sea over the densely forested mountain slope up to the alpine meadows 3000m/9840ft above sea level. At the Pontic foothills there are swathes of virgin forest, rhododendrons and waterfalls. On the higher elevations the volcanic origin becomes evident: between the glaciers you walk lava gravel made of granite. The city dwellers, who are tired of the Mediterranean, come here with their backpacks to hike the mountains and stay at the alpine huts or seek traces of ancient history in the Byzantine churches and Georgian monasteries. The Empire of Trabizond was only defeated in 1461 by Mehmed II the Conqueror. Many Greeks still lived on the northern Black Sea coast into the 1920s. Not only ruins recall the areas dynamic history: in the north-east on the Georgian border about 80,000 Laz (an ethnic group who resisted both the Hellenization and Turkish influences in the north-east) still live. The outermost western Black Sea coast is a popular weekend getaway for Istanbul locals because of its bays and sandy beaches. There has been turmoil in the villages since 2011.

Photo: Tea harvest at the Black Sea coast

Highlands for explorers: tropical climate, lush vegetation and Byzantine monasteries in the east of the Black Sea coast

Since the government adopted a law on the construction of dozens of dams in the region, the residents from the affected areas have gone on the warpath. Large scale logging and ecologically reckless dam building infuriate the activists. On the Black Sea there is also a strong movement against the privatisation of drinking water and the construction of nuclear power plants.

AMASYA

(124 A–B3) (*ⓜ K3*) **This picturesque city (pop. 328,000) in a narrow valley on the banks of the Yeşilırmak (green river) is lined with historic Ottoman timbered houses.**

The pretty setting is completed with Seljuk buildings, mosques and mausoleums as

Unesco World Heritage site: the city of Safranbolu

well as an ⚜ old Roman fortress. Amasya was the capital of the Greek Pontic Empire (circa 300–70 BC) and in Middle Ages the city experienced an economic boom under Mongolians rule. Afterwards the economic centres shifted towards the west. Today the people live mostly from agriculture.

SIGHTSEEING

SULTAN BEYAZIT KÜLLIYESI (MOSQUE COMPLEX)
The complex from the 15th century includes the mosque, mausoleums, fountains and a *medrese*, which is the repository for about 20,000 books. *Ziya Paşa Bulvarı*

FOOD & DRINK

BAHAR RESTAURANT
Known throughout the city for its kebab selection. *Yüzeller Mah. | Sadıkesen Sok. 4 | tel. 0358 2 18 13 16 | Budget*

WHERE TO STAY

BÜYÜK AMASYA OTELI ⚜
This large mid-range hotel is right on the river, with its back to the mountains. The rooms are simple but spacious. Besides excellent cuisine, the restaurant offers great views on to the river and in the summer it also serves guests on the terrace. *50 rooms | Amasya | Nergiz Mah. 1 | tel. 0358 2 18 50 80 | www.buyukamasyaoteli. com.tr | Moderate*

INFORMATION

Mustafa Kemal Paşa Cad. 27 | tel. 0358 2 18 50 02

SAFRANBOLU

(122 C2) *(ᗰ G2)* ⭐ **Cobblestone streets and old timbered houses with indoor water pools make this town (pop. 47,000) an attraction.**
The sale of saffron was the reason for this town's (north of Ankara) prosperity – today handicraft and tourism are the flourishing industries. Safranbolu lies in a deep valley between forested mountains and is a Unesco World Heritage Site. The timbered houses (some very large) are listed buildings and are gradually being restored. A new housing development

on the outskirts of the city provides the residents with modern accommodation whilst they continue their work in the old town. If you rent a car, you can drive into the nearby woods and forests and explore the untouched nature with canyons and beautiful, small rivers.

FOOD & DRINK

BONCUK (ARASTA) CAFÉ
One of the most beautiful traditional coffee houses in Turkey is in a house that dates from the 17th century, in the bazaar district behind the main mosque. In the summer you sit outside under the trees. In the winter a furnace burns in the main room and a buffet is prepared of all the delicious regional dishes. Wonderful selection of fruit teas *(meyve çayı),* and also cappucinos or filter coffee. *Arasta | Yemeniciler Sok. 48 | tel. 0370 712 20 65 | Budget*

SAFRAN
Large restaurant with summer garden, live music at weekends. *Bağlar Aslanlar Meydanı | tel. 0370 712 10 19 | Budget*

SHOPPING

BAZAAR
The town centre is the realm of coppersmiths, sadders and spice traders. Hand-embroidered blankets and cloths are typical of the region.

WHERE TO STAY

INSIDER TIP TOURING SAFRANBOLU HOTEL
Book yourself in to one of the most beautiful mansions in Safranbolu! Decorated in the regional style, with kelims and copper tables; the shady old walnut tree in the garden is delightful. Restaurant in the vaulted cellar. *19 rooms, 5 suites | Çarşı*

Mah. | Ç. Gülersoy Cad. 18 | tel. 0370 712 528 83 | www.safranbolukonak.com | Moderate

INFORMATION

Çeşme Mah. | Arasta Çarşısı 7 | tel. 0370 712 38 63 | www.safranbolu.gov.tr

WHERE TO GO

AMASRA ★ (122 C1) (ω G2)
About an hour's scenic drive from Safranbolu a steep road winds down into the enchanting port city of Amara (pop. 13,000). Located on two rocky headlands, framed by an impressive cliff-lined coast, the ancient Sesamos is one of the crowning jewels of the Black Sea coast. Right on the beach is the basic but clean hotel *Eroğlu Büyük Liman (36 rooms, some with balcony | Kum Mah. | Turgut Işık Cad. | tel. 0378 3 15 39 00 | Budget).* An excellent fish restaurant by the sea is the *Canlı Balık (Büyük Liman Cad. | tel. 0378 3 15 26 06 | Budget).*

★ **Safranbolu**
Browse and buy: attractive timber architecture and the best craft guild souvenirs → p. 82

★ **Amasra**
Cliffs and wonderful bays ideal for swimming → p. 83

★ **Ayder Plateau**
Plateau in the hiking paradise of the magnificent Kaçkar Mountain range → p. 86

★ **Sümela Monastery**
Famous, and massive, cliff monastery that has been hewn into a rock face → p. 87

MARCO POLO HIGHLIGHTS

SİNOP

(123 F1) *(m J1)* **In a picturesque setting on a peninsula and guarded by an imposing, old castle with its city walls, Sinop** INSIDER TIP **has the most beautiful natural harbour on the Black Sea and some wonderful swimming bays and coves nearby.** Founded by colonists from Milet in the 7th century, the city played an important role as a port under the Byzantines. It is famous as the birthplace of the philosopher Diogenes (circa 413 BC) who made a virtue of poverty and lived in a wooden barrel. Even though the city (pop. 198,000) and its surroundings actually meet all the criteria for a pleasant holiday, today almost all the visitors, who fill the cafés and beaches in summer, are locals. The peninsula of Sinop is the most northern tip of the Turkish Black Sea coast and is therefore also a little awkward to get to. There is a ferry from Istanbul (Mon 2pm), which travels back on Thursdays (12.30 from Sinop) contact number in Istanbul: *tel. 0212 2 44 02 07). Turkish Airlines flies daily from Istanbul at 10am (flight takes 1 hour, 20 min / 70–80 lira / www.turkishairlines.com).*

SIGHTSEEING

ARCHAEOLOGICAL MUSEUM
There are interesting objects from early civilisation (including amphorae and coins). Archaeologists suspect the sea in front of Sinop was once inundated by a flood, possibly the Great Flood. *Tue–Sun 8.30am–5.30pm / entrance approx. 3 lira / Okullar Cad. 2 / www.sinopmuzesi.gov.tr*

FOOD & DRINK

BEYAZ EV
The hotel at the sea offers hearty and tasty Turkish cuisine. *Mobil Mevkii / tel.* *0368 2 61 28 66 / beyazevhotel.com / Moderate*

SARAY RESTORAN ⬩⬩
The restaurant at the harbour has one of the best views and excellent Black Sea fish. *İskele Cad. Rıhtım Sok. 18 / Liman / tel. 0368 2 61 17 29 / Budget*

WHERE TO STAY

VILLA ROSE
Five minutes from the sea; this one of the most beautiful small hotels in the region due to its classical furnishings. Small but nice outdoor pool. *5 rooms, 2 apartments / Ada Mahallesi / Kartal Cad. 9 / tel. 0368 2 61 19 23 / Expensive*

ZINOS COUNTRY HOTEL
A new timber-frame building by the sea with private beach. Good, rustic breakfast; in the evenings regional specialities are served. In September the hotel offers fishing trips on the Black Sea – the fish caught is later grilled. You can rent out canoes and hammocks. *Karakum / Ada Mah. Enver Bahadir Yolu 71 / tel. 0368 260 56 00 / www.zinoshotel.com.tr / Moderate*

INFORMATION

İl Turizm Müdürlügü / Vilayet Binası / Kat 4 (4th floor of the town hall) / tel. 0368 2 61 52 07

WHERE TO GO

GERZE
(123 F1) *(m J2)*
Gerze is worth a visit if only for the spectacular 20km/12.4mi trip from Sinop to the village. The road winds steeply through the forest with glimpses of the Black Sea. In the surrounding bays (Bedre, Hurma, Kargasa) the swimming is fantas-

tic. Car rentals and boat tickets at: *Sinope Tours | Kıbrıs Cad. 3 A | tel. 0368 2 61 79 00 | www.sinopetours.com*

HAMSAROZ KOYU (FJORD)
(123 F1) (* J1*)

A fjord (22km/13.6mi from the town centre) that cuts deeply into the coast, its depth and surrounding countryside feel more like Norway than Turkey. There is a forestry administration *(Orman Yeri)* picnic area on the bay, where you can find a wonderful rest place for a minimal fee. In front of the entrance to the fjord there is a beach that stretches for miles.

TRABZON

(125 F2–3) (* N2*) **The old Trabizond in the north-east is today the largest city in the region (pop. 740,000) and – compared to other cities in the east – it is a modern city.**

Until its capture by the Ottomans in 1461, it was the capital city of the Late Byzantine Empire. The most famous sightseeing attraction is the Hagia Sophia from the 13th century, today a museum. The *Trabzon Citadel* (Trabzon Kalesi) rests on a Byzantine foundation, but was later expanded by the Ottomans. Trabzon harbour is an important shipping point for the tea, hazelnuts and wood grown in the area. Trabzon is a conservative city, so you need to pay special attention to how you dress.

> **CITY WHERE TO START?**
> **Atatürk Square:** The town stretches out behind its industrial port, and the square is the best starting point to set out from when exploring the old town. From here you can head out to the mosques, old churches and the city museum. Unfortunately, a wide main road separates the sea from the settlement. You can get to Atatürk Alanı, with its beautiful tea gardens, on foot or by bus or taxi. The airport is quite far outside the city limits in the east.

Scenes from the story of creation: murals in the Hagia Sophia

SIGHTSEEING

AYASOFYA (HAGIA SOPHIA)

The Byzantine church (1238–63) was built by Emperor Manuel I Komnenos and is an important example of Late Byzantine architecture. In 1577 it was turned into a mosque, over time the building had various uses including a depot and clinic, until it became a museum in 1957. The interior is decorated with wall and ceiling paintings depicting the history of creation. *Tue–Sun 8am–midday, 1pm–5pm | entrance 3 lira | Uzun Sok. Zeytinlik Cad. 10*

FOOD & DRINK

BALIKCI DEDE

The 'old fisherman' at the sea serves classic Turkish starters with cornbread followed by small sardines *(hamsi)* fried in corn oil – an enjoyable evening at reasonable prices.

LOW BUDGET

▶ The *Barinak Café* in Sinop harbour is famous for its affordable and delicious pizzas. *İskele Cad. | tel. 0386 2 61 27 18*

▶ Rice with anchovies *(Hamsili Pilav)* is a Trabzon delicacy. For next to nothing you can eat your fill at *Tarihi Kalkanoglu Pilav Salonu. Closed Sundays| Pazarkapı | Tophane Sokak 2*

▶ If you want to discover the Black Sea region on your own, *Thalassa Tours* in Trabzon is a good choice: they have rentals from 70 lira/day. *Gazipaşa Cad. | Saruhan İş Merkezi/ 1st floor| tel. 0462 3 22 11 22 | www. thalassatours.com*

Akyazi | Devlet Karayollari Alti | tel. 0462 221 03 98 | Budget

WHERE TO STAY

ZORLU GRAND HOTEL

Only 4km/2.5mi from the airport, the *Zorlu* is the only five star hotel in the city. Spacious rooms, fitness centre with a sauna and Turkish bath as well as three different restaurants. *160 rooms | 17 non smoking | Maraş Cad. 9 | tel. 0462 3 26 84 00 | www.zorlugrand.com | Expensive*

INFORMATION

Atatürk Alanı | tel. 0462 3 21 46 59 | www. anatolia.com

WHERE TO GO

AYDER PLATEAU ★ (126 B3) (*ω P2*)

The 1350m/4429ft alpine pasture of Ayder is a good point of departure for hikes into the magnificent *Kaçkar Mountains*. The route there starts from Rize on 50km/31mi of good road. The ● INSIDER TIP Berghof Liligum is an excellent place to stay to enjoy the solitude of the mountains, and you can have breakfast at a small waterfall and enjoy some healthy local food. *11 rooms | with bath | Çamlıhemşin Ayder | Aşağı Ambarlık Mevkii | tel. 0464 6 57 21 23 | cell 05374552677 | www.ayderliligum. com*

BILBILAN (126 C2) (*ω P2*)

A high alpine pasture with breathtaking views, on the road from Artvin to Ardanuç (130km/80mi from Rize). From the beginning of June to end of September there is a big INSIDER TIP market in Bilbilan, where you can get practically everything, from livestock to the dairy products that the locals pride themselves on. Only accessible by car (2660m/8727ft). The arduous

Religious seclusion at a lofty height: the cliff monastery of Sumela

drive up the pass from Artvin takes a good two hours. In winter the road is snowed under.

SÜMELA MANASTIRI (SÜMELA MONASTERY) ★
(125 F3) (*∅ N3*)

There are several churches and monasteries in the Pontic Mountains. The most famous and well preserved is the rock monastery of Sümela (270m/886ft high, 50km/31mi south of Trabzon), which was extensively restored by the Turkish Ministry of Culture, in the *Altındere National Park*. The monastery, built right into a cliff face, is a 45 minute walk from a car park. As a good base for hiking tours we can recommend the clean *Büyük Sumela Hotel (115 rooms | Maçka, Trabzon | tel. 0462 5 12 35 40 | www.mackamotel.com | Moderate)* 13km/8mi from the monastery.

Its foundations date back to the 4th century when, according to legend, monks hid Luke the evangelist's icon of the Virgin Mary in the rock cave. The last Greek monks had to leave the monastery in 1923, when Greece and Turkey agreed to a 'population exchange'. The 14th century frescoes in the chapel are unfortunately badly damaged. *Several times daily minibuses from Trabzon harbour or with Usta Tur | tel. 0462 3 26 18 70 (from June)*

UZUNGÖL (LONG LAKE)
(126 A3) (*∅ O3*)

This picturesque lake in the highlands was formed by a landslide that created a natural dam. It is about 80km/49.7mi from Trabzon on the road to Bayburt. The guesthouse with restaurant *Inan Kardeşler (at the southern end of the lake | tel. 0462 6 56 60 21 | Budget)* is the oldest of the dozen restaurants and lodgings on Uzungöl. It has over 22 INSIDER TIP wooden bungalows. *Buses daily from Trabzon/Rus Pazarı Russian market with Çay Kara Otobüsleri*

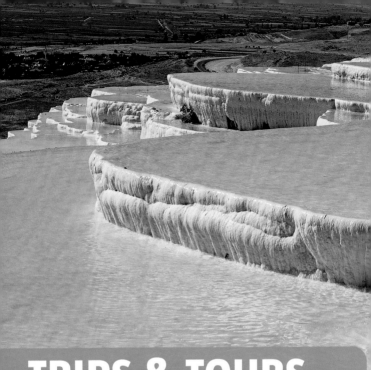

TRIPS & TOURS

The tours are marked in green in the road atlas, the pull-out map and on the back cover

1 HISTORY'S TRAIL IN STONE

Over the centuries settlers, tribes, dynasties and empires have left their imprint on Asia Minor, like the patterns on a Turkish carpet. First the Hittites (2000 BC) came to Central Anatolia, then the Greeks arrived on the west coast in 700 BC and a good 500 years later the Romans took over large parts of modern-day Turkey. This seven day round trip (1800km/1120mi) takes you through the sites from each epoch and some of Turkey's wonderful spectacles of nature.

The starting point is the port city **İzmir** → p. 45, where a walk on the Kordon promenade gives you an impression of the fantastic location of ancient Smyrna. Leave the city and head north on the 550 (E 87) then take the exit to Bergama, ancient **Pergamum** → p. 49. The Greek ruins outside the town are widely spread out, and be warned that the climb up the Acropolis is exhausting. Set aside at least half a day. If you don't want to stay over in Bargama, continue on the 240, then take a small slip road near Kırkağaç, which takes you to the 565 main road towards Balıkesir and a bit further on to **Bursa** → p. 36. The Ottoman Empire's first capital

Photo: Pamukkale's travertine terraces

Go on the trail of the Hittites, up a mountain strewn with statues of gods and down to the beaches: four fabulous journeys of discovery

is located in a fertile river plain, dominated by Mount Uludağ (2543m/8343ft). Stay a night, explore the old town and relax in one of the many acclaimed thermal baths. The next day the route leads you in an easterly direction on the 200 towards Ankara → p. 63. This modern capital city is a good opportunity to do some shopping and to take in a visit to the Hittite Museum.

The world famous collection of the Museum of Anatolian Civilizations fits in well with the next destination: head east on the E 88 until you get to the Delice junction, from there take the 190 to Sungurlu, where a short time later a sign directs you to Boğazkale. Here you can view the temples and gates belonging to the famous Hittite capital Hattusha → p. 66. Together with the nearby rock sanctuary, Yazılıkaya, the

Women in the monastery of the Mevlevi Order of whirling dervishes in Konya

site is a unique open air museum of the first Anatolian civilisations.

From there the trip continues to Cappadocia → p. 66 and the fascinating landscape of 'fairy chimneys'. First drive from Yozgat via the 200, 785 and 260 to Kırşehir and from there on the 765 to Nevşehir in the heart of Cappadocia. The bizarre rock formations – and the remarkable homes, chapels and monasteries carved into them – will simply take your breath away. You have the selection of rock churches of Göreme → p. 66, the fascinating underground cities of Derinkuyu and Kaymaklı → p. 67 or the Peristrema Valley → p. 67, an impressive canyon. Because the sunsets in this landscape are so fantastic, you should definitely stay a night.

From Nevşehir the trip continues further on the 300 past Aksaray to Sultanhanı. Take a rest in the Sultanhanı Kervansaray, the most beautiful of all the surviving Seljuk caravanserais. After 40km/25.8mi you reach Konya → p. 68, a green oasis and the Islamic centre of central Anatolia. The

many Seljuk and Ottoman monuments and the Mevlana Museum of the dervish brotherhood are worth making a day of it.

Pamukkale → p. 49 is the next stop: drive from Konya to Beyşehir (on the 330), from there it is a short stretch along Lake Beyşehir northwards on the 695 and then on 330 via Egidir to Isparta. It then continues to Dinar (685 and 625) and eventually on the 320 to Denizli. Prior to the entrance into the city there is a turnoff to the famous limestone terraces, that were popular thermal baths even in ancient times. Cleopatra visited Pamukkale, to make use of the natural benefits of the mineral-rich water. Enjoy the unique natural thermal baths or you can also go to one of the nearby hotels and make use of their themal facilities. Continue the trip via the 320 and the 550 to the last highlight of the tour, the well preserved ancient city ruins of Ephesus → p. 48. If you still have enough time, visit the nearby seaside resort of Kuşadası → p. 48, before you return to İzmir, the original starting point of this route.

from the sea. It is worth a visit because of the `INSIDER TIP` miles of sand dunes and wetlands of the Göksu river delta and the many beaches in the area. Passing the industrial and port city of Adana the route then takes you via the E 91 to Antakya, the ancient Antioch. The town's Archaeological Museum features an interesting `INSIDER TIP` collection of Roman mosaics. Traces of the first Christians are evident: Peter himself apparently started one of the first churches in a cave (St Peter's grotto).

Şanlıurfa → p. 75, this next stage is heavily influenced by the Arabs and Kurds and you reach this ancient city, founded by the Babylonians, from Gaziantep on the 825 and 400. Its labyrinth-like bazaar of Şanlıurfa – with its coppersmiths and cool tea courtyards – alone makes it worth a visit. Followers of the three largest monotheist religions believe that the founding father Abraham lived for a time in Şanlıurfa and was believed to have been born in a cave at the 17th century Halil-ur-Rahman Mosque. In the last few years massive areas of cotton are being cultivated around Şanlıurfa, this is thanks to reliable water sources from the South-East Anatolian Project and the Atatürk Dam.

The 875 takes you will across the Euphrates, near the gigantic dam, to Adıyaman, the starting point for excursions to the world famous 'mountain of gods' Nemrut Dağı → p. 77. The giant stone heads were part of the tomb for King Antiochus I of Commagene, once the ruler of a small kingdom of Roman nobles. Because the sunrises and sunsets on Mount Nemrut are such a memorable part of your Turkey experience, you should plan to stay overnight. The *Hotel Zeus* is recommended, it is in Kahta close to the start of the climb. *66 rooms | Mustafa Kemal Caddesi 20 | Kahta Adıyaman | tel. 0416 7 25 56 95 | www. zeushotel.com.tr | Moderate*

② BETWEEN BEACH, BAZAAR AND MOUNTAIN GODS

This 1000km/621mi journey gives you a glimpse into the scenic and social contrasts that Turkey has to offer. Leaving modern Antalya, you travel along the eastern Mediterranean coast to Arab influenced Antakya, and from there into the deepest southeast Anatolia, to the Prophet's city of Şanlıurfa and to Mount Nemrut, a mountain of gods. You should allow at least a week for this tour.

From the Turkish Mediterranean metropolis Antalya → p. 53, take the 400 coastal road 135km/84mi eastwards to Alanya → p. 50 ⛱ home of a massive coastal Seljuk fortress with magnificent views.

Now the route follows a winding road to Anamur → p. 52, the southernmost point of Turkey with its 13km/8mi of fine beach and a well preserved ⛱ crusader fortress in a spectacular location. The next stop is Silifke, a district capital 10km/6mi away

THE MOST BEAUTIFUL PART OF THE SOUTHERN AEGEAN IN 48 HOURS

A round trip that takes you to the hustle and bustle of Bodrum and Marmaris, the beautiful bays of the Reşadiye peninsula or the lovely old towns of Milas and Muğla. You should set aside at least two days for the 250km/155mi long route.

You begin the round trip in Marmaris → p. 60. This former fishing village – on one of the largest, sheltered bays on the eastern Mediterranean – has become one of the biggest holiday resorts in southern Aegean. Marmaris is famous mostly for its yacht marina where many tours, also to the Greek islands, set out from. A cabin charter, with several days of adventure at sea, is therefore also an option to consider at this point of the tour. From Marmaris the route takes you overland through the densely forested hills of the peninsula towards Muğla (400), until it joins up with the main coastal road at Gökova.

Gökova is a small village at the end of the gulf (perfect for a swim) before the road to Muğla leaves the sea and winds up 800m/2624ft into the mountains. If you have a day to spare, you should take the coastal road east for 30km/16.5mi, to see Lake Köyceğiz → p. 61, the eponymous village and the holiday resort of Dalyan → p. 61. At Dalyan take a boat trip through the giant reed beds all the way to the beach.

Once in Muğla, the old town is especially worth a visit. Muğla is the capital of the province with the tourist strongholds of Bodrum, Marmaris and Fethiye, but as it is tucked in the mountains, away from the crowds, it has managed to remain unspoilt by tourism.

The next day you leave Muğla and go via Yatağan and Milas to Bodrum. In Yatağan

the government built a coal power plant (despite resistance by the locals) marring the ancient cultural landscape. Despite this, the ancient Roman town of Stratonikai, on the road to Milas, is worth a visit. Milas, the nearest city, is a lively provincial town that serves as the agricultural hub for the coastal communities in the region. There is not much to see in the village itself, but further north on the 525 are several ancient sites, the most famous of which is the ruins of the Temple of Zeus at Euromos, considered one of the best preserved ancient sacral buildings in Turkey.

The route from Milas takes you south-west on the 330 to Bodrum → p. 32. Bodrum itself, and the other holiday resorts along the Bodrum peninsula, are often referred to as the 'St Tropez of Turkey'. Even though there are exclusive, expensive hotels in Bodrum, the city offers enough choice for the 'normal' visitor. Bodrum is especially popular with British tourists and its nightlife is legendary. A landmark is the Crusader castle at the harbour with its spectacular underwater museum.

From Bodrum you take a small ferry, which can only carry a few cars, on the Gökova Gulf which separates the Bodrum peninsula from the Reşadiye peninsula. The peninsula juts out like a finger to the west into the sea. At the top of the finger tip is the ancient Greek city of Knidos. Today you can look out from the ruins of the amphitheatre on to the harbour bay, which was once the source of the city's wealth. The coastal road leads to Datça → p. 61, the small town that is the centre for the fishing and holiday villages of the peninsula. Datça is lively in summer; from the harbour there are ferries to the Greek island of Symi.

The road from Datça leads back to Marmaris over a few hills, from which you have a wonderful view of the open sea and also

Drop anchor where it's pretty: boats in Bodrum harbour

the Gulf of Gökova. Shortly before Marmaris there is the option to make a detour to Bozburun. The secluded sailing harbour of Bozburun is ideal for those looking for a chance to spend a few more quiet days by the sea.

4 A WHISTLE-STOP TRIP TO THE BLACK SEA COAST

This tour takes you to some of the highlights of the eastern Black Sea coast. The valleys and mountains of the Pontic range, the seclusion of the high pastures *(yayla)* and the Byzantine monasteries are all bound to leave a lasting impression: this area shows a very different side to Turkey. The 650km/404mi tour will take about a week, two to four days more if you do some of the hikes.

The journey starts in Trabzon → p. 85, the old Trabizond, where you can visit the ruins of Byzantine and Greek settlements, such as the Hagia Sophia and the citadel. There are some nice tea gardens and restaurants at the harbour. From there you take the 885 via Maçka to the world fa-

mous Sümela Monastery → p. 87. Then you can either drive 43km/26.7mi back and stay overnight in Trabzon, or you continue your route via the fantastic Zigana Pass and Bayburt to Uzungöl → p. 87. After such a long stretch you should stay at this beautiful highland lake before you return on the 2nd or 3rd day, on the 915 along the coast and make a short detour to Sürmene (Tuesday is market day). The town is worth a visit for its 200 year old fortress-like town mansion, built by a Black Sea dynasty, that is an excellent example of regional architecture. From there the tour takes you about 120km/74.5mi further eastwards via Rize and Ardeşen to the Çamlıhemşin (pop. 2000).

From there – at the edge of the Kaçkar Mountains – the route takes you 17km/10.5mi further up into the alpine landscape to Ayder → p. 86. From there you can explore the Kaçkar range in several separate day tours or cross the mountain range in – depending on the conditions – two to four days to Barhal in the province of Artvin (it is best to go with a group). From Ayder it is 160km/99.5mi back to Trabzon.

SPORTS & ACTIVITIES

Even if the favourite destination for package tourists is still the Turkish Riviera, an increasing number of visitors are those seeking an active holiday. Pristine mountains, magical hiking trips and beautiful nature make this country ideal for sports enthusiasts.

BEACHES

The best beaches are on the Mediterranean from Kalkan in the west to Mersin in the east. In 2009 a total of 286 beaches and 14 marinas were awarded Blue Flag status for excellent quality water *(www. mavibayrak.org.tr)*. The beaches on the Black Sea around *Ağva/Şile* and *Sinop* are more secluded, but also cooler than those in the south. In Istanbul you can swim on the Black Sea coast (e.g. *Kilyos*), in the south in *Erdek* and on the islands in the Maramara Sea *(Avşa, Marmara Adası)*. The Aegean coast has mostly pebble beaches or rocky shores. The further south you go, the more sand there is, e.g. around Marmaris *(İçmeler)* or *Ölüdeniz* in Fethiye. The most beautiful beach is *Patara* in the south.

BOAT TRIPS

The beautiful Turkish coast is ideal for a one (or more) week cruise in the southern

Surfing on the coast and skiing in the mountains: with its seas, mountains and rivers, Turkey is a real challenge to sports enthusiasts

Aegean or on the 'Riviera'. Do some Internet research for 'Blue Voyages' boats, schedules and prices. You can charter an entire boat with crew or just a single cabin if that is your preference. *Arya Yachting* has a big selection of boats with experienced crew members *(from approx. 600 lira/week with full board without alcohol. Drinks | Bodrum | Caferpaşa Cad. 25/1 | tel. 0252 316 15 80 | www.aryatours.com).*

DIVING

You can dive in Istanbul, on the Mediterranean and on the Aegean. In Alanya you can try the *Walter Schmidt Diving Base (tel. 0242 5 13 12 96)*. Many beginners go to *Kaş* to get their PADI or CMAS certification, which is offered by several schools with their own boats: *Nautilus Diving | Likya Cad. 1/A | Kaş Antalya | tel. 0242*

8 36 20 85 | www.nautilusdiving.org.
Professionals also dive in the *Dardanelles*
and in the *Gulf of Saros* near Çanakkale
(*Neptün Dalış Merkezi | Büyük Truva Oteli |
Cevat Paşa Mah. | Mehmet Akif Ersoy Cad.
2 | tel. 0286 2 17 10 24*).

GOLF

The facilities in Istanbul and on the Mediterranean coast are very popular with
golfers and the clubs also offer courses.
The *Gloria Golf Club* is a five star hotel complex with its own courses (*18 holes, par
72, 6288m/3,9mi | Acısu Mevkii | Belek/
Antalya | tel. 0242 7 15 15 20 | www.gloria
golf.com*). The 230 acres championship
golf course of the *National Golf Club* has
narrow fairways and is challenging, it and
includes seven water hazards/lakes (*18
holes, par 72, 5569m/3.46mi | Belek Turizm
Merkezi | Serek | tel. 0242 7 25 54 00 |
www.nationalturkey.com*). The *Kemer Golf
& Country Club*, in the Belgrade Forest, is

only 30 minutes away from the centre of
Istanbul (*tel. 0212 2 39 77 70 | www.kemer
country.com*).

MOUNTAIN CLIMBING

Turkey's peaks reach from the highest
mountain Ağrı (Ararat) in the east
(5137m/16,945ft) to the *Taurus Mountains*
(Toroslar) on the Mediterranean and the
Karadeniz Dağları and *Kaçkarlar* along the
Black Sea coast. Smaller mountains like
Kazdağı, Ilgaz, Samanlı, Bolu or *Uludağ*
are ideal for rock climbing and hiking trips.
The Taurus Mountain range is suitable
for hikers in both summer and winter. In
the west are the *Beydağları* and *Akdağlar*
ranges with thousands of peaks that make
good routes for winter hikes and climbs.
In the centre are the *Bolkar* and *Aladağlar*
ranges, separated by the *Gülek Pass*. There
are high mountain lakes, canyons and
caves. On the eastern Black Sea are the
Kaçkar Mountains with peaks such as the

Perfect for thrill seekers: rafting in the Köprülü Canyon

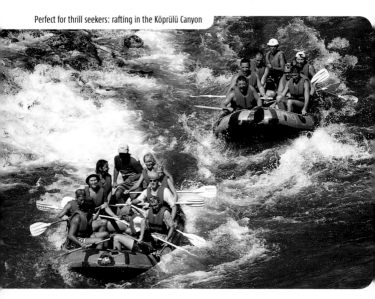

Verçenik (3932m/12,900ft) with its lush green vegetation. A good, affordable service for local mountains tours, also on Mount Ararat, is *Nes Travel Istanbul (General Yazgan Sok.17 | Tünel-Beyoğlu/ Istanbul | tel. 0212 2 44 31 31 | www. nestravel.com)*.

PARAGLIDING

Ölüdeniz/Fethiye: from Babadağ (1700m/ 5577ft) it is a downhill glide all the way. Due to the wind and seaside conditions experienced fliers can stay thousands of feet in the air for up to 5 hours. The long, wide beach is ideal for landing. But beware: accidents do happen! The flight needs to be booked one site the day before *(e.g. Flying Dutchman | tel. 0252 6 17 02 01 | www.flyingdutchman.com.tr)*.

RAFTING

The Turkish rivers are often suitable for rafting throughout the year and there are experienced tour guides leading groups. Swimmers over the age of 14 years are allowed. One of the ten best rafting rivers in the world is the 350km/217mi long INSIDER TIP *Çoruh* which flows into the Black Sea. From dizzying heights its crystal water flows through magnificent canyons, past bears and snow-covered peaks. Hiking and rafting are often combined in the 8 day trips: *Buklamania | Yeni Çarşı Cad. 28/1 | Galatasaray | Istanbul | tel. 0212 2 45 06 35 | www.buklamania.com.* Excursions to the *Dalaman River: Alternatif Outdoor | Marmaris | tel. 0252 4 17 27 20 | www.alternatifraft.com*

RIDING

Whether in exclusive riding clubs or ad hoc at the beach – riding is fun everywhere. In Istanbul there is the very traditional riding club, where you can go as a guest *(Atlı Spor Kulübu | tel. 0216 7 31 39 20)* while on the Mediterranean the *Oranj Ranch (tel. 0242 8 24 62 90 | www. oranjranch.net)* in *Kemer* is ideal.

SKIING

Turkey has some very high mountains, where snow can be 3m/10ft deep. In the north you can go skiing in the *Anatolian Mountains,* the *Taurus Mountains* in the south, on the *Erciyes* and *Ağrı*. 120km/ 74.5mi west of Ankara *Bolu Kartalkaya* has become a popular skiing area with restaurants, indoor swimming pools and nightclubs. *Grand Kartal Hotel | tel. 0374 2 34 50 50 | www.grandkartal.com*
INSIDER TIP *Saklıkent/Antalya:* Let's say it is March and you have been swimming and surfing in Antalya and are already tanned and happy. And then you drive a further 50km/31mi north-west to the Beydağları Mountains. At a height of 2200m/7217ft you suddenly find yourself knee-deep in snow, renting out skis and zooming through a white forest landscape …

TREKKING & HIKING

Two clearly demarcated trails make hiking in southern Turkey an adventure: the 509km/316mi long *Lycian Way* from Fethiye to Antalya and the *St Paul Trail,* which goes from Perge or Aspendos near Antalya to Lake Eğridir. This 500km/ 310.5mi long trail follows the route that Paul took on his missionary journey and in some parts climbs 2200m/7217ft high up in the mountains *(www.lycianway. com)*. Trekking in Cappadocia is an adventure and includes the volcanic valleys of *Kızılçukur, Güllüdere* and *Zindanönü*, the villages built into rock caves and the scenic Damsa Lake.

TRAVEL WITH KIDS

It is not easy to list activities for children in Turkey because children are welcome everywhere! In this child-friendly country you will never find them treated as an annoyance. Here shop owners and waiters will keep the youngsters entertained, whilst you shop or eat in peace and children are often showered with gifts, kisses and affection – until you say 'stop'. Sometimes you will have to do just that!

Tourist establishments always have facilities for children, unless specifically designated for young couples or singles. These include high chairs, nurseries, entertainment activities and children's swimming pools. Holiday villages often offer babysitting services for a small fee. In good hotels on the Mediterranean you will find that the children have so much fun with the other children that you can really relax and enjoy the beach. Do be aware of large swimming pools – which are available at most hotels – as there is often no grate over the pool's drain which can be dangerous. The harsh midday sun is best avoided and you should also avoid buying food from street vendors.

If your child gets bitten by one of the many stray cats or dogs, go to a doctor immediately for a rabies shot. The health system is very good with the exception of a few remote places and all the large

Photo: Children on the beach at Alanya

Children are always welcome in Turkey: from children's clubs to diving courses – here are some of the most interesting activities

hotels have their own doctors. Beware: private clinics are often a money trap!

AROUND ISTANBUL

KEMERBURGAZ/DURUSU
(121 D2) *(ⓜ D2)*

Only 40km/25.8mi away from the busy metropolis of Istanbul is this large recreation area which includes the remains of the Roman-Byzantine aqueduct, which was extended by the master builder Sinan. Stretching over two square miles down to the Black Sea is a comfortable hotel with indoor swimming pool, horse riding with ponies as well as a small railway. Entertainment for children and mountain bikes and canoes for rent. *Durusu Park Resort Hotel | Sales Office: tel. 0212 2 32 41 12 | Hotel: tel. 0212 7 67 90 20 |*

RAHMI KOÇ SANAYI MÜZESI (121 E2) (*m D2*)

This museum – founded by a family of wealthy industrialists – is full of wonderful model ships and trains, real aircrafts, wreckage parts and vintage vehicles. It manages to make the history of technology (from the first astronomical devices through to computers) fun and interesting and it also contains a large quantity of valuable originals. When you try out the controls on the captain's bridge you feel like you really are at sea! Afterwards the children can enjoy the Golden Horn parks. *Tue–Sun 10am–5pm | entrance 12.50 lira | Hasköy Cad. 2 | Hasköy/Istanbul | www.rmk-museum.org.tr*

WEST COAST

CULTURAL PARK İZMIR
(128 B2) (*m B5*)

This extensive park facility is right in the heart of the city, and is lots of fun for children: there is an amusement park and a lake with pedal boats and a host of other amenities. *Free entrance (except during the International Fair from 26 Aug–10 Sept) | İzmir Merkez | Şair Eşref Bulvarı | buses from airport and bus station*

BODRUM'S CRUSADER CASTLE
(128 C4) (*m B6–7*)

Built by the knights of St John in the beginning of the 15th century, not only is this castle is an excellent example of crusader architecture but it is also an inspiring excursion for children: they can climb its many towers and marvel at the crusaders' coasts of arms. It includes the glass wreck hall, an amphora collection, a torture chamber, and Princess Ada's chamber (including a sarcophagus with her remains) and last but not least, the many ancient archaeological and shipwreck finds from Aegean all make this castle a true adventure. *Tue–Sun 8am–midday and 1pm–5pm, in the summer Tue–Sun*

The street as a playground – children in Istanbul

9am–7pm | entrance 12.50 lira | Kale Meydanı | Bodrum

SOUTH COAST

LYKIA WORLD/FETHIYE
(129 E5) (*ω D7*)

Behind the Lycian mountains in a bay covered with pine trees lies this large holiday resort with its own long pebble beach. Its Children's Paradise is one of the best facilities in the Mediterranean area: three heated paddling pools, 15 water slides, adventure caves, a treasure island, water cannons and a pirate's forest. There is also a children's theatre, judo, football, an arts and crafts workshop, skateboarding (July–Oct), trampoline, table tennis and billiards as well as children's courses in swimming, surfing, sailing, tennis and diving. Included in the price is supervision for children from the age of 3 years.

The children head out to the Children's Paradise right after breakfast and there are babysitters available around the clock (for a fee) and prams available with a deposit. The club even offers a kitchen to prepare baby food. Very popular with German and Austrian guests. *PK 102 | Ölüdeniz | Fethiye | tel. 0252 6 17 02 00 | tel. 6 17 04 00 | www.silkar.com/lykia world | www.lykiaworld.org.uk/#childrens paradise*

DIVING WITH CHILDREN
(130 A5) (*ω E7*)

In Antalya, on Tekirova beach, the whole family you can have an exciting diving and beach holiday. The dive centre *Azur* at the ☺ *IFA Beach Hotel* also offers courses for children; but the budding divers have to be at least 10 years old. When the adults explore the wonderful undersea world and caves off shore, the younger ones can either join them or they can do a week-long swimming pool dive course (approx. 260 lira) that comes with a smart display certificate. Snorkelling and diving courses are also offered for adults at the dive centre *Azur* at the hotel: *tel. 0242 8 21 40 46*

BLACK SEA COAST

AĞVA (121 E2) (*ω E2*)

Located about 90 minutes drive from Istanbul, at the confluence of the Yeşilçay and Göksü rivers, on the Black Sea. The village itself is small, but the sea against the mountain backdrop is all the more impressive. Ten minutes walk from the village is the bungalow complex along the Yeşilçay surrounded by orchards, with swimming pool. There are canoes and pedal boats and you can also fish on the river. There is a long, pristine beach at the river mouth: all of which make Ağva an ideal choice for a holiday with children. There are regular buses from Istanbul/ Üsküdar to Ağva. You can stay at the *Riverside Club. Yakuplu Mah. 2 | tel. 0216 7 21 82 93 | umut@riverside.com.tr*

POLONEZKÖY (121 E2) (*ω D2*)

Founded in the middle of the 19th century by Polish immigrants, the 'Polish village' is an ideal rural excursion for children. Its close proximity to Istanbul (only 25km/15.5mi away) means that you can combine your stay in the village with a city holiday. It is glorious in spring when all the flowers and fruit trees are in full bloom and in June you can pitch in and help with the cherry harvest, in winter there is usually snow. There are bicycles to rent and ponies to ride. The *Polka Country* hotel is in a restored timber-frame house *(15 rooms | Cumhuriyet Yolu 36 | tel. 0216 4 32 32 20 | www.polkahotel.com)* and you can enjoy some good food at *Leonardo Restoran (tel. 0216 4 32 30 82)*.

FESTIVALS & EVENTS

Istanbul was named the European Capital of Culture 2010 and it is where most of the events place – including the highly recommended ▶ *Istanbul Music Festival* and the ▶ *Jazz Days*. But also other cities like İzmir or Antalya have caught up. Traditional festivals in the countryside are often modest, but always welcoming. Information about the Istanbul Festival at *www.istfest.org*. Tickets available at *www.biletix.com*.

OFFICIAL PUBLIC HOLIDAYS

1 Jan *Yılbaşı* (New Year); **23 April** *Ulusal Egemenlik ve Çocuk Bayramı* (Festival of National Sovereignty and Children); **19 May** *Gençlik ve Spor Bayramı* (Youth and Sports Day); **30 Aug** *Zafer Bayramı* (Victory Day); **29 Oct** *Cumhuriyet Bayramı* (Foundation of the Turkish Republic)

RELIGIOUS HOLIDAYS

In the Islamic lunar calendar religious festivals move forward eleven days each year
▶ *Kurban Bayramı* (Feast of Sacrifice) the highest Islamic festival lasts four days: 15–18 Oct 2013; 4–7 Oct 2014

▶ *Ramazan* (Ramadan) is the annual month of fasting for Muslims: 9 July–7 Aug 2013; 28 June–27 July 2014
▶ *Ramazan Bayramı* (Sugar Feast) a three day festival that ends the Ramadan: 8–10 Aug 2013; 28–30 July 2014

FESTIVALS

JANUARY
▶ *Camel fights* in Kale/Myra: camels fight and the winner is the one that knocks his opponent down

MARCH
▶ *European Jazz Festival* in İzmir: first week of March *www.iksev.org*
▶ *Newroz:* the Kurdish New Year Festival (21 March) it is now being celebrated throughout the country

APRIL
▶ *International Film Festival in Istanbul:* in the first half of April Istanbul turns into a film city; *www.iksv.org/film*
▶ *International Music Festival Ankara:* annual celebration of international classical music; *www.ankarafestival.com*

From fasting to festivals – in Turkey celebrations and festivals are held all year round – here are some highlights

MAY

▶ *International Theatre Biennial Istanbul* (2014): Shakespeare is often part of the programme; ▶ *Silifke Festival:* on the south coast with local folk dances

JUNE

▶★ *Aspendos Opera & Ballet Festival:* performances with spectacular backdrop – an ancient Roman amphitheatre *www.dobgm.gov.tr;* ▶ *Istanbul International Music Festival:* classical music in exclusive locations such as the Hagia Irene church at Topkapı Palace; *www.iksv.org;* ▶ INSIDER TIP *International Festivals in İzmir:* classical music in ancient Ephesus is a once in a lifetime experience! *www.iksev.org*

JULY

▶ *Kırkpınar Güreşleri:* outdoor traditional wrestling near the Bulgarian border *www.kirkpinar.com*

▶ *International Jazz Days* in Istanbul *caz.iksv.org/en*

SEPTEMBER/OCTOBER

▶★ *Istanbul Biennial* (2013, 2015): one of most important exhibitions of contemporary art in Europe; ▶ *Antalya Piano Festival:* for six days virtuosos play in the open air *www.antalya.bel.tr*

NOVEMBER

▶ *Efes Pilsen Blues Festival Istanbul:* with many well known American musicians *www.efespilsen.com.tr*

DECEMBER

▶★ *Şeb-i-Aruz:* whirling dervishes in Konya perform their meditative dance on the anniversary (12 Dec) of the death of the founder of the Order; On Christmas Day (25 Dec) a ▶ INSIDER TIP *mass* is celebrated in St Peter's grotto (Antakya)

LINKS, BLOGS, APPS & MORE

LINKS

▶ www.kultur.gov.tr The Ministry of Tourism and Culture introduces the country and its tourist attractions (English/Turkish)

▶ www.turkishculturalfoundation.org A good resource with sections on Turkish music, cuisine and events

▶ www.goturkey.com A website full of information about Turkey's history, nature and climate, culture and lifestyle as well as an interactive map

▶ www.hotelguide.com.tr The ultimate Turkish hotel portal that provides a search facility according to theme and a great deal of information about special offers in each region

▶ www.spottedbylocals.com/istanbul A site that allows you to experience Istanbul just 'like a local' and contains regularly updated tips by hand-picked locals who are passionate about their city

▶ www.i-escape.com/turkey/guide A portfolio of beautiful boutique hotels, private homes and guest houses that also includes some quirky and interesting options. Browse listings according to categories such as 'Foodie', 'Eco' or 'Cheap & Chic'

▶ www.lycianturkey.com This part of Turkey was home to the ancient Lycians — one of the most enigmatic people who were culturally distinct from the rest of the ancient world. Around twenty major sites remain today with the Lycians' unusual funerary architecture dominating this breathtakingly unspoiled area

Regardless of whether you are still preparing your trip or already in Turkey: these addresses will provide you with more information, videos and networks to make your holiday even more enjoyable

BLOGS & FORUMS

▶ http://adventuresinankara.com An award winning blog by an American lawyer who has relocated to Ankara. With musings, recipes, photography as well as a 'Travel Tips' section for visitors

▶ www.turkeytravelplanner.com An online guide with FAQ and guidance about where to go and what to do. Very user-friendly and highly informative

VIDEOS

▶ www.youtube.com/user/TurkeyTourismOffice Some excellent videos on a wide variety of Turkish tourist sites, cities and activities including special interest ones such as 'Blue Voyages' and 'Rafting'

▶ www.5min.com/Video/Visit-Alanya-in-the-Turkish-Riviera-255972229 Video in English focusing on Alanya and with links to other similar videos such as Istanbul, Cappadocia and Pamukkale

APPS

▶ Cruising the Mediterranean App ideal for planning the perfect cruise or yacht trip with information about all the Mediterranean cruise liners, sailing routes, harbours and their infrastructure as well as shore visits

▶ Turkey's Mediterranean Coast App with travel information: maps, planning, safety, health, addresses

NETWORK

▶ www.tripwolf.com Travel tips, photos, blogs and evaluations from the travel community. Background reports and the possibility of direct bookings for accommodation and activities

▶ www.lonelyplanet.com/thorntree Forum not only for tourist travel but also with information about work possibilities. Post your own evaluations, photos and reports

▶ www.airbnb.com Airbnb Is the popular site for travellers who prefer to stay in private accommodation offered by locals. A search under Istanbul pulls up the full spectrum from a deluxe triplex villa through to a studio on the Bosporus. The site is constantly updated with new listings and user reviews

TRAVEL TIPS

ARRIVAL

✈ Most holiday-makers arrive by plane. You can reach any airport in Turkey (either directly or with a stopover in Istanbul) with Turkish Airlines *(www.turkish airlines.com)* as well as other major airlines including British Airways *(www.british airways.com)* and budget operators such as easyJet *(www.easyjet.com)*.
Turkish Airlines also has flights to all the larger cities and are non-stop charter flights throughout the year to Istanbul, İzmir and Antalya, as well as to Dalaman and Bodrum in the high season. The cost of flights varies considerably depending on the season and destination: it is worth spending some time comparing prices or consulting with your local travel agent. And remember that charter companies are always very strict with their luggage limits!

🚗 If you intend to drive, plan your route carefully and inform yourself about the countries you have to pass through, customs formalities and other regulations. Motoring organisations may be able to help. You can drive via Zagreb, Belgrade, Sofia but it is more advisable to take the Hungary-Romania route – or drive to Italy and cross to Turkey by ferry (see below).

⛴ If you have enough time, a trip by ferry from Venice or Brindisi and Bari can be a pleasant alternative. The fare is around £1200/$1850 including car, cabin and full board *(www.feribot.net | www. ankertravel.com)*. One of the nicest routes is from Piraeus through the Greek islands on the Aegean coast *(ferries-turkey.com)*.

🚆 Trains depart from London for Istanbul every day except Christmas Day. The London–Istanbul train journey may cost much more than an air fare, but it is a 3 day adventure, during which you can rediscover some of the mystery and romance of long distance sleeping car travel across Europe.

RESPONSIBLE TRAVEL

It doesn't take a lot to be environmentally friendly whilst travelling. Don't just think about your carbon footprint whilst flying to and from your holiday destination but also about how you can protect nature and culture abroad. As a tourist it is especially important to respect nature, look out for local products, cycle instead of driving, save water and much more. If you would like to find out more about eco-tourism please visit: *www.ecotourism.org*

BANKS & MONEY

Opening times: 9am–midday and 1pm–5pm, in large cities often all day and until 6pm. Branches with the *Öğlen Açik* sign do not close for lunch and branches in shopping centres often have longer opening hours. You can withdraw money from cash dispensers using your EC or credit card. For trips to smaller places you should have enough cash on hand an a few smaller notes. Many shops and restaurants, and almost all hotels, accept the major credit cards. If you want to do a currency exchange, go to one of the special exchange

From arrival to weather

Holiday from start to finish: the most important addresses and information for your trip to Turkey

offices *(döviz bürosu)* where you will receive a better rate than at a bank. It is best not to exchange money before you leave home – the rate is always better in Turkey.

BUSES

The Turkish bus routes reach into the furthest corners of Turkey, unlike the trains. But reduce your risk of being in an accident by avoiding the cheaper offers! The *Ulusoy* and *Varan* bus companies utilise modern tour buses; and on longer routes the drivers change regularly. The prices are so good that you can even book two seats for one person (e.g. İzmir–Antalya 33.50 lira, Ankara–Trabzon 48 lira). *Ulusoy | tel. 0212 65 83 00 01 (24 hrs) | www.ulusoy.com.tr | Varan | tel. 0216 3 36 96 10 or 0212 2 51 74 74 (24 hrs) | www.varan.com.tr*

CAMPING

The best campsites are the state-run 'Forest Camps' *(Orman Kampı)* supervised by the Ministry of Forestry. They can generally be found in shady woodland and have good facilities including telephone, kiosk and shop, places to cook, a laundry, showers with hot water and wastewater disposal for motorhomes and caravans. *www.camping.info*

CAR HIRE

The large suppliers also have branches in Turkey but it is cheaper to rent a car at one of many smaller car rental companies (from about 40 lira/day for a small car including mileage). The vehicle is collected with an empty tank and is returned the same way. When signing a contract, you have to write out a blank cheque for security reasons, which is torn up when the vehicle is brought back. *www.rentacarrehberi.com*

CUSTOMS

There is no limit to the amount of Turkish and foreign currency that can be brought into the country. However, you must pre-

BUDGETING

Coffee	£1.60/$2.50	
	for a cup of coffee	
Tour bus	£23.50/$37	
	from Istanbul to Bodrum	
Snack	£1.20/$1.80	
	for a kebab	
Beer	£1.20/$1.80	
	for a bottle of beer in a restaurant	
Hammam	£20/$31	
	for a visit	
Petrol	from £1.60/$2.50	
	for 1L Super	
Taxi	£0.50/$0.80	
	per kilometre	

sent a receipt for any carpets or other articles of value purchased in Turkey. Be careful about buying genuine antiques: as a rule, items that are more than 100 years old cannot be exported. And it is strictly forbidden to take ancient stones and other antiques out of the country. This also applies to fossils. Even articles that you bought cheaply from a street trader can cause enormous problems.

DOLMUŞ

Travelling by shared taxi, *dolmuş* (pronounced dolmoosh), is very economical. They are small buses that take specific routes and stop wherever passengers

CURRENCY CONVERTER

£	TRY	TRY	£
1	2.80	1	0.35
3	8.40	3	1.05
5	14	5	1.80
13	36.50	13	4.50
40	112	40	14.50
75	210	75	27
120	335	120	43
250	700	250	90
500	1400	500	180

$	TRY	TRY	$
1	1.80	1	0.55
3	5.40	3	1.65
5	9	5	2.75
13	23	13	7
40	71	40	22
75	135	75	41
120	215	120	66
250	445	250	138
500	890	500	275

For current exchange rates see www.xe.com

want to jump on or off. The prices in the city vary from 1 to 6 lira. In large holiday resorts like Marmaris, Bodrum, Fethiye, Alanya or Side there are also *dolmuş* buses in the surrounding areas. If you want to get a ride to a beach, the buses often depart at fixed times, so you should make inquiries beforehand. But you can also get stuck in a *dolmuş* in the midday heat waiting for the departure!

DRIVING

To enter the country driving your own car you will need your driving license and registration and insurance papers. It is also important take out partial or full comprehensive insurance and passenger cover for Turkey. A police report is required for any claims.

The speed limits: in residential areas 50km/h, outside 90km/h and on motorways 130km/h. There is a total ban on driving after you have consumed alcohol. Maps and tips for drivers are available from the *Turkish Touring and Automobile Club, TTOK (Türkiye Turing ve Otomobil Kurumu) 1. Oto Sanayii Sitesi Yani | 4. Levent | Istanbul | tel. 0 212 2 82 81 40 | www.turing.org.tr*.

TTOK has a breakdown service on the route Edirne–Istanbul–Ankara as well as İzmir–Ankara.

ELECTRICITY

The current in Turkey is 220 volt AC. Adapters are not necessary.

EMBASSIES & CONSULATES

BRITISH EMBASSY
Şehit Ersan Caddesi 46/A | Çankaya, Ankara | tel. +90 (0)312 4 55 33 44 | uk inturkey.fco.gov.uk/en

BRITISH VICE-CONSULATE ANTALYA
Gürsu Mahallesi | 324. Sokak No: 6 | Konyaaltı, Antalya | tel. +90 (0)242 4 22 28 28 11 | ukinturkey.fco.gov.uk/en

CANADIAN EMBASSY ANKARA
Cinnah Caddesi no. 58 | 06690, Cankaya | Ankara | tel. +90 (0)312 4 09 27 00 | www.canadainternational.gc.ca/turkey-turquie

CANADIAN CONSULATE ISTANBUL

209 Buyukdere Caddesi | Tekfen Tower, 16th Floor | Levent 4, Istanbul | tel. +90 (0)21 23 85 97 00 | www.canadainter national.gc.ca/turkey-turquie

US EMBASSY ANKARA

110 Atatürk Blvd. | Kavaklıdere 06100 | Ankara | tel. +90 (0)31 24 55 55 55 | turkey. usembassy.gov

US CONSULATE ADANA

Girne Bulvari No: 212 Guzelevler Mah. Yüregir | Adana | tel. +90 (0)32 23 46 62 62 | adana.usconsulate.gov

Other embassies and consulates can be found under *embassy.goabroad.com/ embassies-in/turkey*

Police: *tel. 155*; fire brigade: *tel. 110*; emergency doctor: *tel. 112*

Tap water is not suitable for drinking but plastic bottles of still *(su)* and carbonated *(soda)* water are sold everywhere.

You will be treated free of charge in the state hospitals (SSK Hastanesi) if you have your EU health insurance card. However, it is less complicated and more convenient to take out travel insurance before you leave home; private clinics are usually better equipped. In pharmacies *(eczane)* you can get a lot of common medication cheaper than back home, and often without a prescription. However, there are sometimes supply shortages: if you need chronic medication, it is highly recommended to bring ample supply from home.

A comprehensive list of hospitals and doctors in the region can be found on the British Embassy website *(ukinturkey.fco. gov.uk/en)*.

A multiple-entry, sticker-type visa, valid for three months, can be obtained at any point of entry into Turkey for a fee: UK citizens: £10 (Important: Payments in pounds must be in Bank of England £10 notes only. No Scottish or Northern Irish notes and no other values of notes, i.e. £5 or £20); US citizens: US$20; Canadian citizens: US$60. *More Information: www. mfa.gov.tr/consular-info.en.mfa*

Tourism offices in Turkey are called *Turizm Bürosu*.

TURKISH CULTURE & TOURISM OFFICE

*Fourth Floor | 29–30 St James's Street | London SW1A 1HB | tel. 020 78397778 | www.gototurkey.co.uk
2525 Massachusetts Ave. | Washington, DC 20008 | tel: (202) 612-6800 | 821 United Nations Plaza | New York, NY 10017 | tel. (212) 687-2194 | tourismturkeysite.com*

INTERNET

www.istanbulcityguide.com has event information, tickets are available at *www. biletix.com.*
www.hotelguide.com.tr shows you the accommodation available throughout Turkey.
www.bigglook.com/biggtravel is an informative travel website in English

Turkey offers free wireless Internet and Wi-Fi hotspots almost everywhere. Most hotels offer free ADSL and Wi-Fi in the rooms or at least in the lobby. In holiday resorts almost every café has the Internet, and you only have to request the access code. Due to all this public access, it is not recommended to do your bank transactions from your hotel room or from a coffee table! Internet cafés are also in almost every corner of Turkey. Surfing the net costs about 3 lira per hour.

– Ankara: Argos | Tandoğan, Mebusevleri | Anıt Cad. 14/5 | tel. 0312 2 15 63 94 | www. argoscafe.com
– Antalya: Sanal Alem | Kazım Özalp Cad., Beşinci Sok. 2 | tel. 0242 2 44 56 70 | www.sanal.osmanli.com
– Bodrum: Bodrum Internet Café | Oasis Shopping Mall | tel. 0252 3 17 00 22 | guras@superonline.com
– Diyarbakır: Nokta | Ekinciler Cad. Kışla Sok. 18 | tel. 0412 2 29 25 96 | www. diyarbakir.com
– Istanbul: Orient Hostel | Sultanahmet | Akbıyık Cad. 13 | tel. 0212 5 18 07 89 | www.orienthostel.com

PERSONAL SAFETY

When planning your travel you should review the current security situation in the region. Up-to-date information is available on foreign affairs websites such as, *travel. state.gov* (US) and *www.fco.gov.uk/en* (UK).

PHONES & MOBILE PHONES

The Turkish telecommunications is a state affair and phone calls home are expensive! Between 8pm and 6am night rates apply. Prepaid phone cards are available in post offices and in kiosks *(telefon karti)* for public phone boxes. Cheaper still are the prepaid service cards: you rub away the number on the card and dial via a service number, where you first have to

enter your secret code and then your international number.

Mobiles are very common in Turkey and there is good reception countrywide. Mobile phones from abroad are subject to roaming charges and these can be expensive.

PHOTOGRAPHY

It is strictly prohibited to take photographs of military and police personnel and buildings (including bridges and harbours). You should also not take photographs of veiled women. If one is not explicitly prompted to take a photo, you should respect dismissive hand movements.

POST

Turkey no longer has post boxes; you leave your letters and postcards at the hotel reception or at the post office (PTT). Offices are usually open from 8am–5pm on weekdays.

PRICES & CURRENCY

The unit of currency is the Turkish lira (TRY). There are 5, 10, 20, 50, 100 and 200 lira notes as well as 1lira and 10, 25 and 50 *kuruş* coins. Admission fees change very often due to the relatively high rate of inflation. Turkish visitors sometimes pay a lower price than foreign tourists.

TAXI

Travelling by taxi is relatively inexpensive but you must insist on the meter being turned on, don't be fooled by specials! And never take a taxi without having some change in your pockets; if you only have high denominations it may be awkward for the driver. From midnight–6 am in many places (not in Istanbul!) there is a night tariff (50% more). In smaller places a higher basic fee is charged due to shorter routes. Beware of people trying to trick you, who try to give you a 5 lira note instead of a (very similar) 50 lira note when giving you change – look a carefully at the notes, and check the amount!

TIME

Turkey is one hour ahead of Central European Time and 2 hours ahead of GMT. The same applies to daylight saving periods which are the same in Turkey as in the rest of Europe.

TIPPING

A ten per cent tip is commonplace – and expected – in restaurants and hotels. When paying for a taxi ride, you can round up.

WEATHER & CLIMATE

The best time to travel to Turkey is from April to the end of October. The summer at the Mediterranean is very hot, in the Anatolian highland and in east Turkey the heat is also very dry. Winter, on the other hand, means lots of snow and icy cold. In winter, which can stretch into April, there is also often snow in Istanbul. The weather at the Black Sea is often cloudy and humid.

WEATHER IN İZMİR

	Jan	Feb	March	April	May	June	July	Aug	Sept	Oct	Nov	Dec
Daytime temperatures in °C/°F	12/54	14/57	16/61	21/70	26/79	30/86	33/91	33/91	29/84	24/75	19/66	14/57
Nighttime temperatures in °C/°F	5/41	5/41	6/43	10/50	14/57	18/64	21/70	21/70	17/63	14/57	10/50	7/45
Sunshine hours/day	4	6	6	8	10	12	13	12	10	8	6	4
Precipitation days/month	12	9	7	6	4	1	0	0	1	4	6	11
Water temperatures in °C/°F	15/59	13/55	14/57	15/59	18/64	21/70	23/73	23/73	22/72	20/68	17/63	16/59

USEFUL PHRASES TURKISH

PRONUNCIATION

ı	like 'a' in 'ago', e.g.: ırmak
c	like 'j' in 'jump', e.g.: cam
ç	like 'ch' in 'chat', e.g.: çan
h	like English 'h', or 'ch' in Scottish 'loch', e.g.: hammam
ğ	a silent letter than extends the vowel before it, e.g.: yağmur
j	like 's' in 'leisure', e.g.: jilet
ş	like 'sh' in 'ship', e.g.: teker
v	like 'v' in 'violin', e.g.: vermek
y	like 'y' in 'young', e.g.: yok
z	like 'z' in 'zoom', e.g.: deniz

IN BRIEF

Yes/No/Maybe	Evet/Hayır/Belki
Please/Thank you	Lütfen/Teşekkür (ederim) or Mersi
Excuse me, please!	Afedersin/ Afedersiniz
May I ...?	İzin verir misiniz?
Pardon?	Efendim? Nasıl?
I would like to .../Have you got ...?	... istiyorum/... var mı?
How much is ...?	... ne kadar? Fiyatı ne?
I (don't) like that	Beğendim/Beğenmedim
good/bad	iyi/kötü
broken/doesn't work	bozuk/çalışmıyor
too much/much/little	çok fazla/çok/ az
all/nothing	hepsi/hiç
Help!/Attention!/Caution!	İmdat!/Dikkat!/Aman!
ambulance	ambulans
police/fire brigade	polis/itfaiye
Prohibition/forbidden	yasak/ yasak

GREETINGS, FAREWELL

Good morning!/afternoon!/	Günaydın/İyi Günler!/
evening!/night!	İyi Akşamlar!/İyi Geceler!
Hello! / Goodbye!	Merhaba!/Allaha ısmarladık!
See you	Hoşçakal (plural: Hoşçakalın)/
	Bye bye!

Türkçe biliyormusun?

"Do you speak Turkish?" This guide will help you to say the basic words and phrases in Turkish.

DATE & TIME

Monday/Tuesday/Wednesday	Pazartesi/Salı/Çarşamba
Thursday/Friday/Saturday	Perşembe/Cuma/Cumartesi
Sunday/working day	Pazar/İş günü
Holiday	Tatil Günü/Bayram
today/tomorrow/yesterday	bugün/yarın/dün
hour/minute	saat/dakika
day/night/week	gün/gece/hafta
month/year	ay/yıl
What time is it?	Saat kaç?

TRAVEL

open/closed	açık/kapalı
departure/arrival	kalkış/varış
toilets / ladies/gentlemen	tuvalet (WC) / bayan/bay
Where is ...?/Where are ...?	Nerede ...?/ neredeler ...?
left/right	sol/sağ
straight ahead/back	ileri/geri
close/far	yakın/uzak
bus/tram/underground / taxi/cab	otobüs/tramvay/metro / taksi
bus stop/cab stand	durak/taksi durağı
parking lot/parking garage	park yeri/otopark
train station/harbour/airport	istasyon/liman/havaalanı
schedule/ticket	tarife/bilet
single/return	tek gidiş/gidiş dönüş
train/track	tren/peron
I would like to rent ...	... kiralamak istiyorum
a car	bir otomobil/araba
a boat/rowing boat	bir tekne/sandal
petrol/gas station	benzin istasyonu
petrol/gas / diesel	benzin/dizel
leaded/unleaded	kurşunlu/kurşunsuz
breakdown/repair shop	arıza/tamirhane

FOOD & DRINK

Could you please book a table for tonight for four?	Lütfen bize bu akşama dört kişilik bir masa ayırın.
on the terrace/by the window	terasta/pencere kenarında
The menu, please	menü lütfen

Could I please have ...?	... alabilir miyim lütfen?
bottle/carafe/glass	şişe/karaf/bardak
knife/fork/spoon	bıçak/çatal/kaşık
salt/pepper/sugar/vinegar/oil	tuz/karabiber/şeker/sirke/zeytinyağı
milk/cream/lemon	süt/kaymak/limon
cold/too salty/not cooked	soğuk/fazla tuzlu/pişmemiş
with/without ice	buzlu/buzsuz
Water sparkling/still	su/soda
vegetarian/allergy	vejetaryan/alerji
May I have the bill, please?	Hesap lütfen
bill/receipt/tip	fatura/fiş/bahşiş

SHOPPING

Where can I find...?	... nerede bulurum?
I'd like .../I'm looking for ...	... istiyorum/... arıyorum
Do you put photos onto CD?	CD'ye fotoğraf basıyor musnuz?
pharmacy/chemist	eczane/parfümeri
baker/market	fırın/pazar
shopping centre/department store	alışveriş merkezi/bonmarşe
grocery/supermarket	gıda marketi, bakkal/süpermarket
100 grammes/1 kilo	yüz gram/bir kilo
expensive/cheap/price	pahalı/ucuz/fiyat
more/less	daha çok/daha az

ACCOMMODATION

I have booked a room	Bir oda rezervasyonum var
Do you have any ... left?	Daha ... var mı?
Single bed/single room	tek yataklı/tek kişilik oda
Double bed/double room	çift yataklı/çift kişilik oda
breakfast/half board/	kahvaltı/yarım pansiyon/
full board (American plan)	tam pansiyon
at the front/seafront	ön tarafta/denize bakan
shower/sit-down bath	duş/banyo
key/room card	anahtar/oda kartı
luggage/suitcase/bag	bagaj/bavul/çanta

BANKS, MONEY & CREDIT CARDS

bank/ATM	banka/ATM
pin code	şifre
I'd like to change ...	... bozduracağım
cash/credit card	nakit/kredi kartı
bill/coin	banknot/demir para
change	bozuk para

USEFUL PHRASES

HEALTH

doctor/dentist/paediatrician	doktor/diş doktoru/çocuk doktoru
hospital/emergency clinic	hastane/acil doktor
fever/pain	ateş/ağrı
diarrhoea/nausea/sunburn	ishal/bulantı/güneş yanığı
inflamed/injured	iltihaplı/yaralı
plaster/bandage	yara bandı/gazlı bez
ointment/cream	merhem/krem
pain reliever/tablet	ağrı kesici/hap

POST, TELECOMMUNICATIONS & MEDIA

stamp/postcard/letter	posta pulu/kartpostal/mektup
I need a phone card	Bir telefon kartı lazım
I'm looking for a prepaid card	Bir hazırkart lazım
Where can I find internet access?	İnternete nereden girebilirim?
dial/connection/engaged	çevirmek/hat/meşgul
socket/adapter/charger	priz/adaptör/şarj aleti
computer/battery/rechargeable battery	bilgisayar/pil/akü
internet connection/wifi	internet bağlantısı/wireless
e-mail/file/print	(e-)mail (e-posta)/dosya/basmak

LEISURE, SPORTS & BEACH

beach/bathing beach	sahil/plaj
sunshade/lounger	(güneş) şemsiye(si)/şezlong
low tide/high tide/current	med/cezir/akıntı

NUMBERS

0	sıfır	15	on beş
1	bir	16	on altı
2	iki	17	on yedi
3	üç	18	on sekiz
4	dört	19	on dokuz
5	beş	20	yirmi
6	altı	21	yirmi bir
7	yedi	50	elli
8	sekiz	100	yüz
9	dokuz	200	iki yüz
10	on	1000	bin
11	onbir	2000	iki bin
12	oniki	10000	on bin
13	on üç	½	yarım
14	on dört	¼	çeyrek

NOTES

ROAD ATLAS

The green line ▬▬ indicates the Trips & Tours (p. 88–93)
The blue line ▬▬ indicates The perfect route (p. 30–31)

All tours are also marked on the pull-out map

Photo: Çeşme beach

Exploring Turkey

The map on the back cover shows how the area has been sub-divided

SH MARITIME LINES

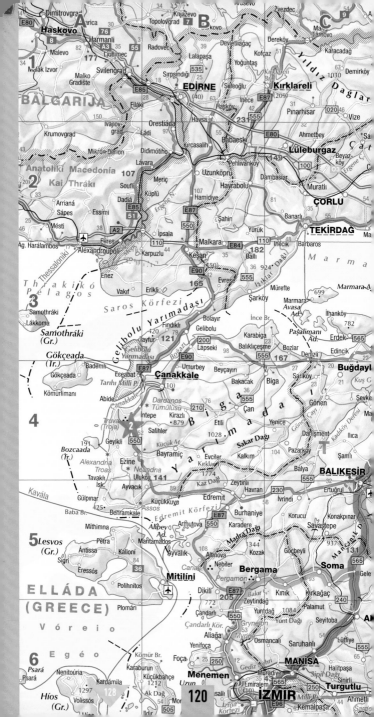

D E F

1

50 km
31.1 mi

K A R A D E N I Z

2

Yalıköy
Karacaköy
Karaburun
Kumköy
Çayağzı
Alacalı
Şile
Ağva
Kefken
Pazarbaşı Br.
Çatalca
Boyalık
Kemerburgaz
Yeşilvadı
Teke
Akcaova
Kandıra
Ziamet
Yeniköy
Esenyurt
BEYKOZ
Ömerli
020
Mollafeneri
Kaynarca
Ferizli
650
Soğuksu
Büyükçekmece
100
FATİH
BAKIR-
KÖY
ÜSKÜDAR
SULTANBEYLİ
KARTAL
304
Kocaeli
Yarımadası
Sevindikli
Akmeşe
605
Söğütlü
İSTANBUL
Büyük Ada
95
GEBZE
Gene Dağı
647
İZMİT
(KOCAELİ)
E80
SAKARYA
(ADAPAZARI)

3

Büyük
Ada
Darıca
Hereke
İzmit
Kör.
Sapanca
Karapürçek
140
D e n i z i
Yalova
130
Karamürsel
Bahçecik
Gölcük
Doğançay
Geyve
İmralı
Ad.
Armutlu
Çınarcık
Kılıç
595
Yalıkdere
Boz Br.
Karaçalı
S a m a n
D a ğ l a r ı
150
Pamukova
25
Gemlik-Körfezi
Zeytinbağı
575
Orhangazi
İznik
Sakarya
C.
Taraklı
150
Göv
Kara Dağ
833
Esence
Mudanya
142
575
Gürsu
Boyalıca
Nikaia
İznik Gölü
Kaynarca
Osmaneli
Gölpazarı
160
DIRMA
Nilüfer Ç.
Sölöz
650

4

E90
200
Uluabat Gölü
100
Hasanağa
Yenişehir
Bilecik
Söğüt
Yeni
163
220
Miletopolis
Çalı
225
BURSA
2543 Uludağ
Milli P.
Uludağ
İNEGÖL
E90
Pazaryeri
152
İnhisar
Sarıc
Mustafakemalpaşa
Söğütalan
Soğuk-
pınar
Tahtaköprü
200
Bozüyük
Boz Dağı
1371
Sündiken Dağları
Susurluk
Devicikonağı
Orhaneli
Keles
Domaniç
İnönü
ESKİŞEHİR
Durak
Kavacık
80
Büyükorhan
Harmancık
Burhan
595
Dodurga
Kümbet

5

230
Dursunbey
Kireç
Gökçedağ
Dağardı
Tavşanlı
Köprüören
Sabuncu
Seyitga
Alaçam Dağları
Civanlı
Opanözü
595
1569
Enne
Türkmen D.
1829
Büyüksaka
Kırka
Bigadiç
Ulus Dağ
1769
Çamlık
Eşatlar
KÜTAHYA
909
240
Düvertepe
2089
Emet
Hisarcık
Örencik
240
Aslanapa
Çavdarhisar
Döğer
650
Yapıldı
Simav
Dağları
1425
Şaphane D.
Aizanoi
97
Keçiler
Altıntaş
İhsaniye
Güneşli
Simav
240
37 2121
Eski Gediz
Arslanta

6

Gördes
Yarbasan
Pazarlar
Abide
Gediz
Murat Dağı
2312
Başkomutan
Gazı
Köprübaşı
585
98
Çamsu
Karabeyli
Dumlupınar
Tarihi
AFYON
Borlu
Enecler
300
Banaz
115
Sınanpaşa
10243
Selendi
595
UŞAK
Demirköprü
Barajı
Kula
E96
Yenişehir
Güre
906
Ahat
Flaviopolis
Hocalar
Karadirek
650
Milli Parkı
Şuhut
Ilıhlı
300
216
Selçık
Sivaslı
Umurbaba D.
129
Sandıklı

121

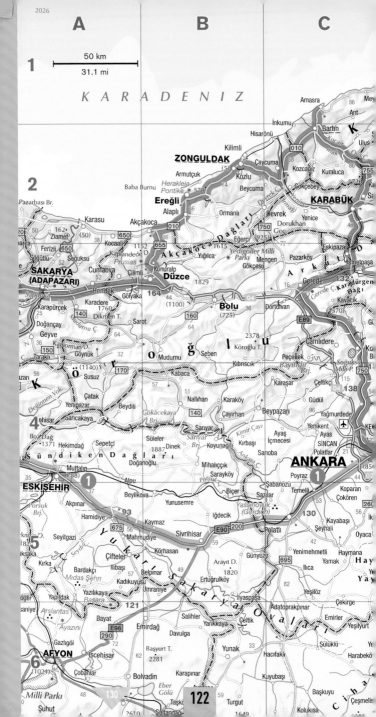

KARADENIZ

A **B** **C**

50 km
31.1 mi

Amasra
İnkumu
Hisarönü
Bartın K
Ulus
Kilimli
ZONGULDAK
010
Çaycuma
Kozcağız Kumluca
755
Armutçuk
Kozlu
Gökçebey
Baba Burnu *Herakleia* Beycuma
Pontike 570
KARABÜK
Ereğli
Alaplı Ormanlı
Devrek
Pazarbaşı Br.
Karasu
Akçakoca Yenice
Dorukhan
Karsu 010 Eğerci 750 Geç
Ziamet (50) Kocaali Ağarköy 925
Ferizli 650 Soğuksu 1152 655 Yığılca Yedigöller Milli Eskipazar İsmetpaşa
Söğütlü 52 Konuralp *Prusias* Pazarköy
SAKARYA Cumaova Çilimli Düzce Mengen Gerede Ç. Kavacık
(ADAPAZARI) Hendek Gölyaka 164 1829 Gökçesu Gerede 132 570
Karapürçek Karadere 164 Bolu Dörtdivan
140 Dikmen T. (1100) 160 (725) Çamlıdere
Doğançay Sarot 64 E89
Geyve 64 2378
150 Kıbrıscık Köroğlu T. Peçenek
Taraklı Göynük O ğ l u Karaşar Çeltikçi 750
Ö r Mudurnu Seben 138
Susuz Kabaca Güdül Yağmurdede
Çatak 170 57 51 Yenikent
Yenipazar Nallıhan Karaköy Beypazarı Ayaş SİNCAN
Sarıcakaya Beydili 140 İçmecesi
Boz Dağ Süleler Çayırhan ANKARA
1371 Hekimdağ Sepetçi Sarıyar Kırbaşı
Sündiken Dağları Dinek 1887 Koyunağılı Sanoba
Muttalip Doğanoğlu Mihalıççık Poyraz
ESKİŞEHİR Alpu Sarıköy Şabanözü Koparan
Akpınar Biçer Temelli Çökören
Beylikova Yunusemre Sazlar 260
Hamidiye 93 Iğdecik 130
Seyitgazi 675 Kaymaz Kayabaşı Oyaca
Çifteler Mühmudiye Sivrihisar E90 200 Polatlı Şyhali
Kırka Körhasan 59 42
Bardakçı İlbası Belpınar Günyüzü Yenimehmetli Haymana
Midas Şehri Kadıkuyusu Arayıt D. 695 Yamak
Yazılıkaya Umraniye 1820 Ertuğrulköy İlıca
Basara İlyaspaşa 82 Yeşilöz
121 Salihler Adatoprakpınar Çekirge
Bayat Yarıkkaya Çeltik Emirler
AFYON E96 Emirdağ Davulga Yunus Süllüklü Harabeköy
290 Başyurt T. Hacıfaklı
İscehisar 2281 Karapınar Kuyubaşı
Çobanlar Bolvadin *Eber* Başkuyu Çeşmelis
Milli Parkı 130 *Gölü* 122 Turgut Kolukısa
Şuhut Sultandağı 1649

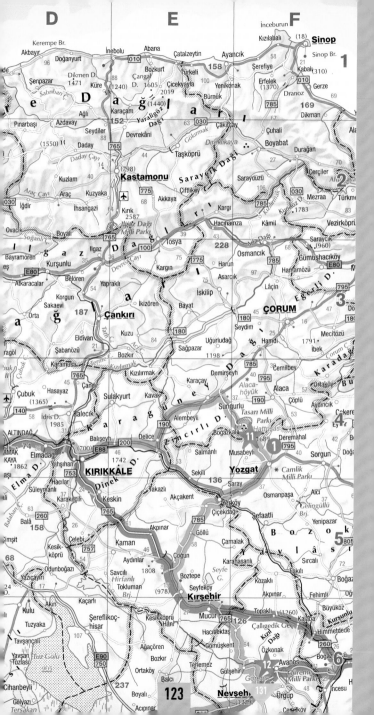

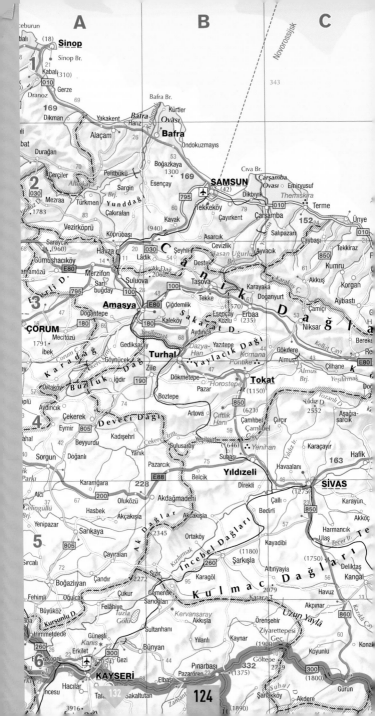

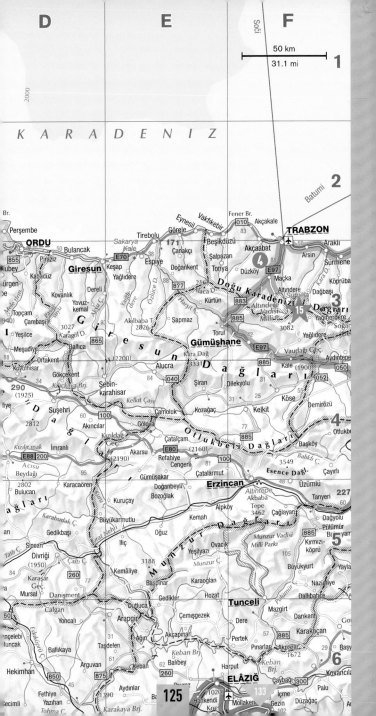

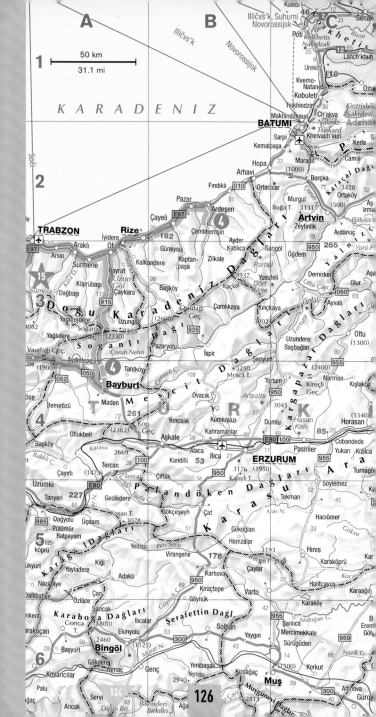

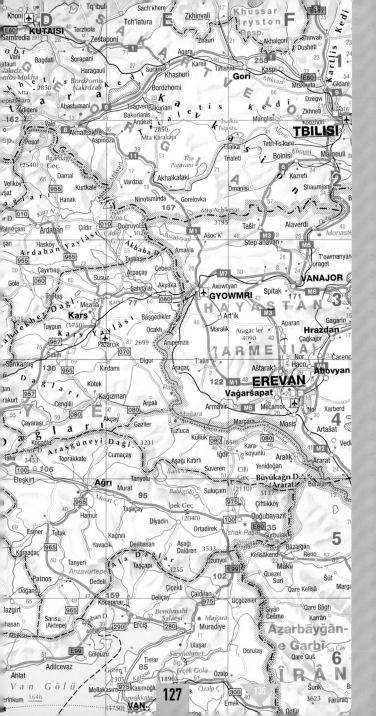

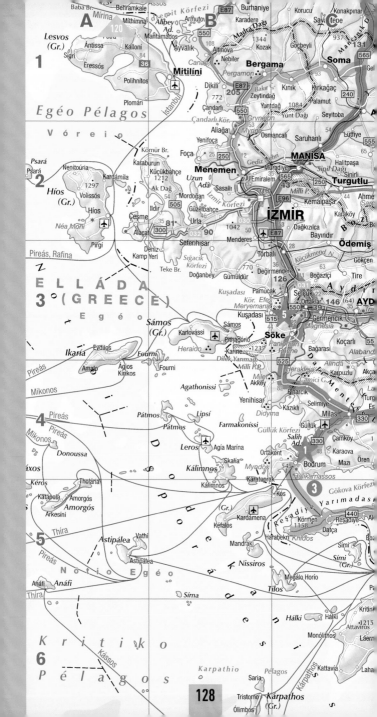

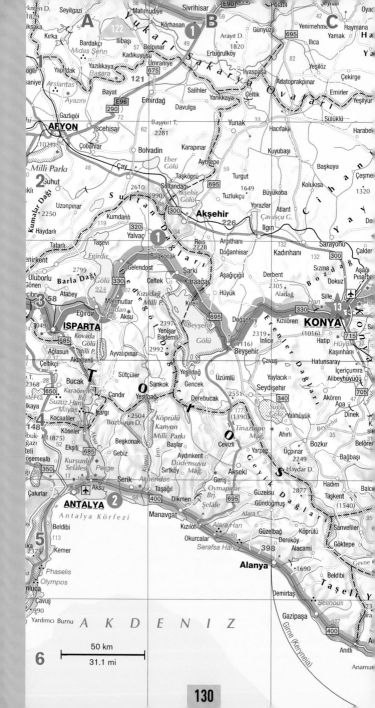

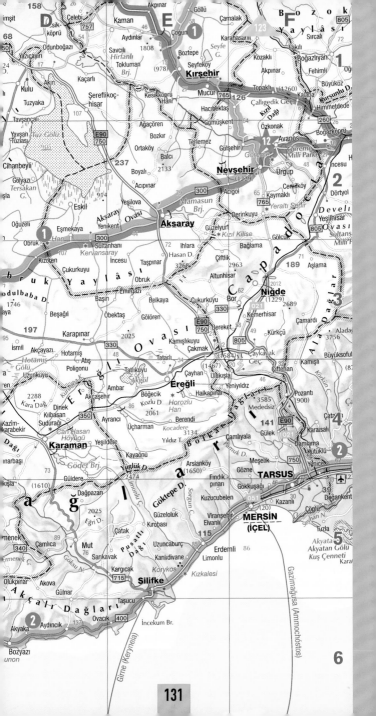

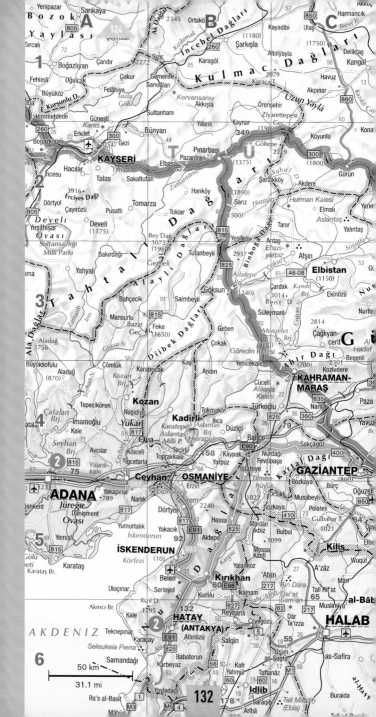

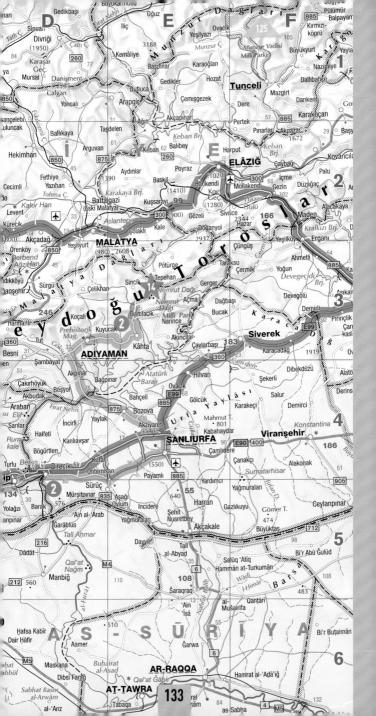

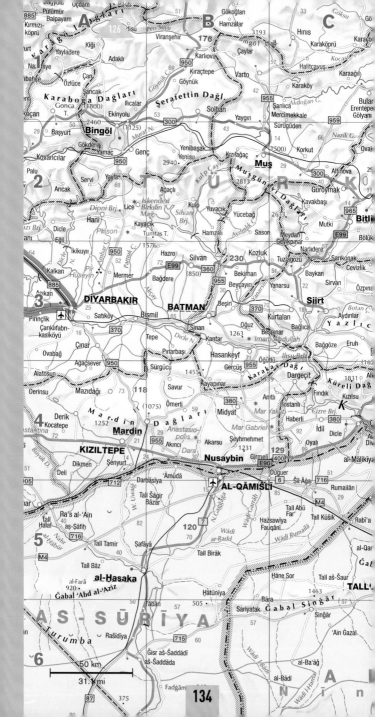

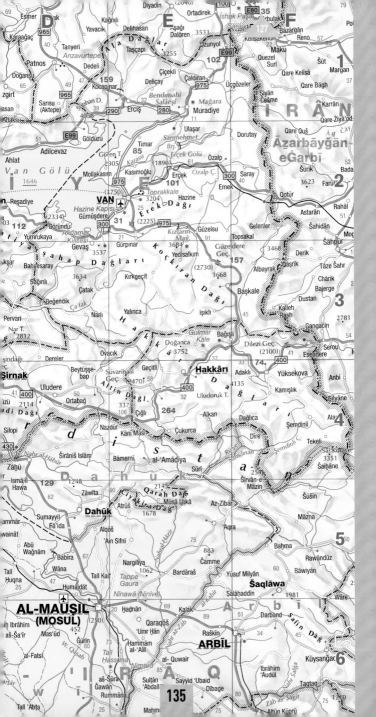

KEY TO ROAD ATLAS

Highway, multilane divided road - under construction Autobahn, mehrspurige Straße - in Bau	≡≡≡ = = =	Autoroute, route à plusieurs voies - en construction Autosnelweg, weg met meer rijstroken - in aanleg
Trunk road - under construction Fernverkehrsstraße - in Bau		Route à grande circulation - en construction Weg voor interlokaal verkeer - in aanleg
Principal highway Hauptstraße		Route principale Hoofdweg
Secondary road Nebenstraße		Route secondaire Overige verharde wegen
Practicable road, track Fahrweg, Piste		Chemin carrossable, piste Weg, piste
Road numbering Straßennummerierung	E20 11 70 26	Numérotage des routes Wegnummering
Distances in kilometers Entfernungen in Kilometer	**259** 130 129	Distances en kilomètres Afstand in kilometers
Height in meters - Pass Höhe in Meter - Pass	1365 •	Altitude en mètres - Col Hoogte in meters - Pas
Railway - Railway ferry Eisenbahn - Eisenbahnfähre		Chemin de fer - Ferry-boat Spoorweg - Spoorpont
Car ferry - Shipping route Autofähre - Schifffahrtslinie		Bac autos - Ligne maritime Autoveer - Scheepvaartlijn
Major international airport - Airport Wichtiger internationaler Flughafen - Flughafen	✈ ✈	Aéroport importante international - Aéroport Belangrijke internationale luchthaven - Luchthaven
International boundary - Province boundary Internationale Grenze - Provinzgrenze		Frontière internationale - Limite de Province Internationale grens - Provinciale grens
Undefined boundary Unbestimmte Grenze		Frontière d'Etat non définie Rijksgrens onbepaalt
Time zone boundary Zeitzonengrenze	-4h Greenwich Time -3h Greenwich Time	Limite de fuseau horaire Tijdzone-grens
National capital Hauptstadt eines souveränen Staates	**OSLO**	Capitale nationale Hoofdstad van een souvereine staat
Federal capital Hauptstadt eines Bundesstaates	**Nancy**	Capitale d'un état fédéral Hoofdstad van een deelstat
Restricted area Sperrgebiet		Zone interdite Verboden gebied
National park Nationalpark		Parc national Nationaal park
Ancient monument Antikes Baudenkmal	∴	Monument antiques Antiek monument
Interesting cultural monument Sehenswertes Kulturdenkmal	* Chambord	Monument culturel interéssant Bezienswaardig cultuurmonument
Interesting natural monument Sehenswertes Naturdenkmal	* Gorges du Tarn	Monument naturel interéssant Bezienswaardig natuurmonument
Well Brunnen	‿	Puits Bron
Trips & Tours Ausflüge & Touren		Excursions & tours Uitstapjes & tours
Perfect route Perfekte Route		Itinéraire idéal Perfecte route
MARCO POLO Highlight	★1	MARCO POLO Highlight

INDEX

This index lists all places and destinations, plus the names of important people and key words featured in this guide. Numbers in bold indicate a main entry